IMAGES of America

MILWAUKEE'S FOREST HOME CEMETERY

Forest Home Historians. The authors for this book are pictured here. From left to right are (first row) Margaret M. Berres and Anita M. Pietrykowski; (second row) Robert L. Giese, Paul A. Haubrich, and Thomas A. Ludka. (Forest Home Cemetery Collection.)

On the Cover: The Blatz mausoleum was constructed in 1901–1902 as the final resting place for beer baron Valentin Blatz. Blatz had died four years earlier, and his wife commissioned this mausoleum as a final memorial. Reportedly, it is made of 500,000 pounds of granite with an Italian marble interior. At the time of its construction, it was considered to be the largest in the Midwest. More can be found in chapter two. (Forest Home Cemetery Collection.)

IMAGES
of America

MILWAUKEE'S FOREST HOME CEMETERY

Forest Home Historians and
the Forest Home Historic Preservation Association

ARCADIA
PUBLISHING

ISBN 978-1-4671-0489-0

Published by Arcadia Publishing
Charleston, South Carolina

Printed in the United States of America

Library of Congress Control Number: 2019954559

For all general information, please contact Arcadia Publishing:
Telephone 843-853-2070
Fax 843-853-0044
E-mail sales@arcadiapublishing.com
For customer service and orders:
Toll-Free 1-888-313-2665

Visit us on the Internet at www.arcadiapublishing.com

Forest Home Cemetery will celebrate its 170th anniversary in 2020. It has taken the work and dedication of thousands to achieve this distinction for continued success.

Contents

ACKNOWLEDGMENTS

Our writing team, the Forest Home Cemetery Historians, would like to thank Jan Van Rens, executive director of Forest Home Cemetery, for her thoughtful encouragements and support over the past 10 months. Her insights and participation in the early stages of this project are much appreciated.

We are also grateful for the support of the Forest Home Historic Preservation Association, the 501(c)(3) that is dedicated to the preservation of Forest Home Cemetery as Wisconsin's premier historic cemetery, and the board of directors for their support. The cemetery staff, office and grounds, has always been supportive of our tour programs and our individual requests for assistance over the years in compiling the information for this book as well as our tours.

Special thanks to Lee Matz, cemetery board member and photographer, for his assistance in preparing some of the photographs used in this book.

Images in this volume have been used with permission. We gratefully acknowledge the following people and organizations for their support:

AMP	Anita M. Pietrykowski
FG	Find A Grave
FHC	Forest Home Cemetery Collection
GSWS	Girl Scouts of Wisconsin Southeast
JMA	James M. Aubery
LM	Lee Matz Collection
MB	Margaret M. Berres
MCHS	Milwaukee County Historical Society
MPM	Milwaukee Public Museum
NG	Nancy Gettelman
PM	Pabst Mansion
RLG	Robert L. Giese
WBHS	Wisconsin Black Historical Society
WVM	Wisconsin Veterans Museum

INTRODUCTION

A BRIEF HISTORY OF FOREST HOME CEMETERY

In 1847, St. Paul's Episcopal Church leaders began discussions for developing a "cemetery for the city." Milwaukee had six small cemeteries, one Catholic, one Lutheran, one Jewish, and three operated by the city. The religious cemeteries restricted burials to members of related religious organizations. The city cemeteries were poorly maintained and were used for grazing animals, and at times the graves were not dug deep enough, causing caskets to rise to ground level. It was in response to these poor conditions that, in 1849, St. Paul's bought 72 acres two miles outside the city limits as a cemetery for a "peaceful rest" that would be open to all. A sales slogan used for decades described Forest Home as "open to all faiths and not-for-profit."

In the spring of 1850, St. Paul's solicited 50 prominent Milwaukeeans to pay $20 each for future burial rights to a family lot of 20 feet by 20 feet, raising $1,000 of operating capital. It contracted with Increase Lapham to design the cemetery. It appears that Lapham was familiar with Mount Auburn Cemetery in Cambridge, Massachusetts, the first of the "garden cemetery" designs in the United States. The basic principle of the garden cemeteries was to maintain the natural landscape and beautify the grounds as a place of dignified burial. Forest Home property reflects the gently rolling countryside that was present when the first settlers came to Milwaukee along with a landscape familiar to the Indian tribes that lived in the area. Evidence of Lapham's design can be seen in the roads that curve throughout the cemetery to follow the rolling landscape.

The first burial at Forest Home was Orville Cadwell on August 5, 1850. One of the early design elements of the cemetery was family lots of 4, 6, 8, and 12 grave spaces. The idea that families would stay together in death was common throughout the Victorian era, only changing to "mom and pop" lots at the time of World War I.

Forest Home benefitted from the rapid growth of Milwaukee both prior to and following the Civil War. When the cemetery opened in 1850, Milwaukee had about 20,000 inhabitants; by 1900, the population had swelled to 285,000 and was still growing. As the city and surrounding communities grew, so did Forest Home by acquiring additional land. By 1900, it reached its current size of 189 acres. Original plans called for families to maintain the family lots, plantings, and grass, but this proved to be impractical, and the cemetery developed a perpetual care charge for property maintenance. This policy allowed for a future revenue stream based on set-asides from each sale being placed into a perpetual care fund—in essence, a type of endowment for the cemetery.

A major problem for any cemetery in colder climates is frozen ground in the winter months. Bodies had to be stored in facilities like root cellars where constant temperature kept them cold until warmer weather allowed for burial. With the increasing use of embalming by the 1880s, storage for bodies over the winter months became easier, and the in-ground storage spaces were removed and repurposed.

Staffing at Forest Home changed dramatically over the years. In the late 1800s, Forest Home had a summertime staff of 40-plus people to cut grass, plant flowers, and dig graves. Today, the cemetery grounds crew consists of eight people for the summer months. The development of power equipment has changed the job dramatically. For years, the cemetery had grave diggers in its workforce, and it could take a team of two men one full day to dig one grave. Today, a backhoe can do it in about one hour. The last grave digger at Forest Home was let go in 1947.

In his book *Silent City*, Milwaukee historian John Gurda calls Forest Home Cemetery Milwaukee's first park. The cemetery was a manicured, peaceful space, and a Sunday ride to the cemetery was considered a treat; families would bring a picnic lunch as part of the trip. Cemetery records report that visitors on sunny days in the late 1800s numbered somewhere between 6,000 and 8,000.

The end of the Civil War began an industrial age in America, and the greater Milwaukee area benefitted from this growth. This led to significant accumulation of wealth, which allowed for the display of significant monuments. Equally important was the newfound ability to cut granite, a durable stone. Cemeteries that existed before the Civil War frequently had gravestones made of marble and limestone; these softer stones deteriorate over time. If you visit older cemeteries, you will see many monuments that are no longer legible and in a state of decline. The popularity of all things Egyptian established a stylish trend of using obelisks, sarcophagi, urns, and other elements to shape the design of these new monuments. What is amazing is that all this granite was pulled into place with horses as the major source of power (see page 117). The Blatz mausoleum, discussed in the Beer Barons chapter, was brought to the cemetery by horse and wagon. The construction crew used a small steam engine to help lift tons of granite into place. In Forest Home, as well as other garden or monumental cemeteries, the race was on to see who could have the biggest and most stunning memorial marker.

In the Victorian era, a variety of symbols were used in the design of larger family monuments, including angels, doves, lilies, wreaths, upside-down torches, and many other subtle signs. This is discussed in more detail in the opening chapter.

During the first 50 years of the cemetery's existence, practices changed considerably. In 1850, burial was generally completed within five days of a person's death. Commonly, the body was displayed in the living room or parlor of the deceased's home for three days, with family and friends visiting to pay their respects. Cemetery processions from either the house or church were generally large and took considerable time, as the cemetery was on the outskirts of the city, and travel by buggy or walking occupied much of the day.

One of the problems with home visitation was the placing of both the casket and the body in the parlor. Generally, the casket was brought in first, and then the body was carried into the house in a wicker casket. When the visitation was over, the process would be repeated, with the body carried out in the wicker basket. This led to the popular phase "Going to hell in a handbasket."

In the 1800s, coffins were preferred by undertakers over caskets. A coffin has six sides, and a casket has four. Today, caskets are used almost exclusively.

An early problem for many cemeteries was collapsed graves. This occurs when the casket, generally wood, deteriorates and collapses around the body, causing a depression in the ground above. Frequently, cemeteries had to bring in additional dirt and grass seed to bring the grave space up to grade.

Embalming gradually became the standard for most burials after the Civil War. The large number of casualties and lack of federal cemeteries posed a challenge for the federal government during the war. Bodies had to be shipped home to their families for burial, which required embalming. Forest Home has two Civil War sections, and there are 1,100-plus Civil War veterans buried here.

Funeral homes did not develop as a common element of the final disposition until the late 1880s. Forest Home maintained its office in downtown Milwaukee, and most property sales occurred there instead of at the cemetery. This was accomplished by viewing a map of the cemetery and looking for property, hopefully close to friends and family. A copy of the 1872 map is displayed in Forest Home's Halls of History. This map also exists as a book that unfolds and can be displayed at the home of the family, saving them a trip to the cemetery.

In the early days, the record-keeping system was a simple alphabetical listing of name and location. It soon became apparent that this was not sufficient as more property and burials were recorded. The cemetery developed a section-and-plot system that precisely identified every grave in a section (see page 116). Once a lot was purchased, the cemetery made a lot card that detailed the number of graves on the lot and the location of each burial by name and year of interment. Each lot is required to have a representative who can authorize burials at that location. Commonly, this is a member of the family. This allows for precise location, with each section, plot, and grave having a number that can be attached to a name. This, coupled with an alphabetical listing, allows cemetery staff to easily find grave locations. Today this has all been computerized, but the section-and-plot map system is still in place.

In 1890, Forest Home contracted with the architectural firm of Ferry and Clas to design a cemetery chapel for funerals and visitations. This chapel, still in use, was unique in its floral conservatories on each side for the display of funeral flowers as well as a seasonal display of flowers. In 1895, Forest Home installed the first crematory in the upper Midwest in the basement of the chapel with both a retort room and a family waiting room.

Many of the early cremations were from out of state. The family would have a service in the chapel and then go downstairs to assist in placing the casket—generally made of pine—into the retort chamber and wait until the cremation was completed. This allowed the family to take the cremains home for disposition. The original crematory remains intact and is open for special viewing events but is no longer used, as newer standards for cremation necessitated the construction of a new facility elsewhere on the cemetery grounds.

Today, cremation has become a popular alternative to traditional burial, with the cemetery offering aboveground placement of an urn in columbaria both indoors and outdoors. Other options include interment on a single grave for two or three cremations as well as a scattering option.

Modern burial options fall into three categories: in-ground, above ground, and indoors. In-ground options are traditional grave burials or placement of a cremation in either a special space or on the grave of a family member. Above ground consists of an outdoor mausoleum for a full casket or placement of cremains in a niche that is part of the outdoor mausoleum. Indoor options are placement of a full casket inside a building or an urn in a cremation niche located inside.

The newest option is called "green burial." This approach requires that the body be cleansed, wrapped in cloth, and placed in a wooden or cardboard casket. The site has no headstone and generally uses a type of prairie grass or other plantings to create a natural look. This type of burial is considered to be friendly for the environment.

Forest Home's history reflects the changes in Milwaukee and its surrounding communities. It is the final resting place for beer barons, industrialists, mayors, governors, senators, and families who have made significant contributions to and helped build Milwaukee. It is also the final resting place for the working people whose contributions provided the labor to build this city.

Today, Forest Home Cemetery is an open and active cemetery with 117,000 buried and burials continuing almost daily. Remarkably, the cemetery still has enough land to continue burials for another 100 years!

—Paul A. Haubrich

One

Cemetery Art and Symbolism

Cemeteries have stories to tell, and at Forest Home Cemetery there are many ways that individuals and families tell something about themselves and their lives. But we have to know what symbols mean to understand what a monument can tell us.

Some are very evident and popular, like the Christian cross, and others are more subtle, requiring some translation to understand. Many lots were sold as family lots of 4, 8, 12, and 16 spaces that generally required a large family marker with smaller individual headstones. These larger family markers were influenced by a number of design elements that are repeated throughout the cemetery in small or large versions.

Symbolism extends to a variety of topics or images that convey mourning, work, achievement, military service, fraternal organizations and societies, hobbies, and expressions of one's standing in society. The rapid growth in the use of larger monuments was due to the rapid growth of wealth in America during the industrial era following the Civil War.

Egyptian designs frequently used are obelisks, some decorated with draped urns, and sarcophagi. Some of the largest obelisks are solid pieces of granite 16 to 24 feet in height. These large sections of granite were brought to the cemetery with an eight-horse hitch from the railroad depot a few miles away.

Other designs are clearly influenced by religious belief, such as the Christian cross and three-step bases on monuments signifying the Trinity. Use of the wreath as a symbol of victory of life after death is also a Christian symbol. An angel is frequently used to signify the person's entrance to heaven along with the dove of peace and lilies to signify purity.

By the end of World War I, the use of large monuments with symbolic meanings began to rapidly be replaced with more simplified markers with dates of birth and death. The end of World War I signaled the end of the period of enlightenment associated with the 1800s and a reduction of the high style of the Victorian era.

—Paul A. Haubrich

Section 6. The Gutknecht family marker is a good example of the symbolism used on many Victorian-era monuments. Here is a woman in mourning, with her head down and covered by a shroud. Many people think this is an angel, but she has no wings. She is holding a wreath, a symbol of victory, in this case victory over death—eternal life. The monument is on a three-step base signifying the Trinity: God the Father, God the Son, and God the Holy Ghost. In the foreground are individual scroll-style headstones of family members. The scroll is an adaptation of the image of a person entering heaven and St. Peter looking at a scroll or book to see if the person's name is on it. If the name is on the scroll, the person will get into heaven. (FHC.)

SECTION 37. This sarcophagus-style marker is for Henry Payne, an industrial leader and postmaster general of the United States from 1902 to 1904. Note the use of the wreath across the front of the marker and the stylized lid. The large front surface allows for his achievements to be made known to all. The last line of his story reads, "After life's fitful fever he sleeps well," suggesting a life lived well. (FHC.)

SECTION 33. This is one of the most ornate sarcophagus-style family monuments in the cemetery. It bears the name of T.L. Hansen. Thomas Hansen was the owner of a storage company that eventually became a moving and storage business. (LM.)

Section 32. This view from the 1920s shows three large obelisks. The closest belongs to Harrison Ludington, lumber baron, mayor of Milwaukee (1871–1876), and governor of Wisconsin (1876–1878). The middle one belongs to George Brumder, publisher of German books, newspapers, and magazines. The distant obelisk is that of William Luick, an ice cream maker who realized that home refrigeration allowed for the packaging of ice cream in smaller pint-sized containers. Luick sold his business and patent rights to the pint container to Sealtest Ice Cream Company, allowing for national distribution. (FHC.)

Section B. This is an older section of the cemetery. Note the many small obelisks used as markers. Many of these were made of marble or sandstone, softer types of stone that deteriorate in harsh weather. Granite as a preferred stone for cemeteries did not become popular until after the Civil War, and many older stones are not easily read, as the stone slowly erodes away. (LM.)

Section 36. The angel seen here is clearly defined by the wings. Monuments with women in mourning are often thought to depict angels, but they must have wings to be angels. Frequently, stone carvers used the same image for a woman in mourning and an angel, thus the confusion. (LM.)

Section 33. This is the family monument of Timothy Chapman (1824–1892), born in Vermont. Arriving in Milwaukee in 1856, he started a dry goods store that developed into Milwaukee's finest department store. The store was on the southeast corner of Wisconsin Avenue and Milwaukee Street. The angel on the front was designed by Thomas Chester French, an American sculptor who is famous for the Lincoln statue at the Lincoln Memorial in Washington, DC. This monument and angel make a wonderful pairing of styles at this family lot. (FHC.)

Woman in Mourning. Women in mourning are common images in the cemetery. The woman here is on top of the Pfister family monument in a typical pose, with her head down. There are no images of men in mourning in the cemetery. It is speculated that many women survived their husbands and wanted to demonstrate the loss. (FHC.)

Section 33. This woman is not in a standard mourning pose; she is very stylized and reaching for the urn at the top of the monument. This unusual image is very sensual compared to other monuments with women in mourning. (LM.)

SECTION 34. This is a Bedford tree stone for the John Phillips (1852–1891) family. The broken tree trunk and branches are symbols of a life lost and may also contain elements of a person's life. This tree contains elements of gardening, including flower pots and garden tools, as well as a relief carving of Phillips. Bedford tree stones are named after a quarry in Beford, Indiana, where the stone was carved. They were frequently used by members of the Modern Woodmen of America, a fraternal benefit organization founded in 1803. The tree motif is also used for headstones and grave markers. (FHC.)

SECTION 17. The Schuster family marker is also a Bedford tree stone. It has Christian symbolism, and behind the larger marker is a smaller tree stone—almost a stump—with a train engine carved on it. For years, it was thought that Frank Schuster must have been a train engineer, but his obituary indicated that he had fallen off the top of a boxcar as the train was moving. Children really enjoy the train stone. (FHC.)

Pillow Headstones, Section 8. Shown here are the Kapanke-Ebner lot (left) and the Hoffman-Bauer lot. Both families used a family monument with "pillow" style headstones for each member. The pillow style is very common at gravesites after the 1880s as a way of signifying peaceful rest. Both lots hold two families; in both, a family member has married a member of the other family, thus leading to two names on the family monuments. (LM.)

Section 6. An unusual style of marker is called the "unfinished life." The marker appears to be only partially finished and contains elements of the person's life. This is the Gerlach family marker. Found on the stone are a cross, a dove, and a lily, all symbols associated with Christianity. The dove is a symbol of peace, and the lily means purity. Notice the scroll symbols for the individual markers. (FHC.)

SECTION 27. From 1850 to 1900, infant mortality rates were very high, at times exceeding 50 percent. The symbolism for infant and childhood deaths is varied. Children who were stillborn were not named and are generally represented on a marker as "Babe" or with a lamb mounted on a marker with no name. Older children were named, with symbols of either a lamb or a child reclining in a bed, as seen here. This marker reads, "Neddie 8 mos. And 14 days." Neddie Allen (1872) was one of four children born to the William Allen family; all are buried at Forest Home. (LM.)

SECTION 32. The two boys shown here are Georgie and Willie Mitchell, sons of Alexander Mitchell, discussed in chapter four, who died at seven months and almost two years of age, respectively. The marker is located behind the family sarcophagus-style marker. (FHC.)

SECTION 6. Urns were very popular in the Victorian era and were frequently placed on top of small, stylized obelisks. The urn is Greek in origin and was originally used for cremains. A draped urn suggests the rending of clothes at the death of an individual, an ancient style of mourning. Some urns have a flame on top, suggesting eternal life for the family members. (FHC.)

SECTION 8. This is the marker for Mathias Stein, Milwaukee's first gun maker. The rifles carved on the monument tell what he did as a career. Notice that there is also a carved image of Stein on the marker. Its accuracy is open to speculation, but it is probably very stylized. His gun shop was on East Water Street in the general location of the current BMO Harris Bank. (FHC.)

SECTION 9. The fireman's hat is a clear symbol of this person's occupation. It tells the story without any speculation as to his career. This is the final resting place of Otto Nimmer. The marker reads, "His Last Call." (FHC.)

SECTION 37. Greek-style columns are frequently found on monuments. In the Victorian era, artists would use the image of a Greek temple to signify the entrance to heaven. The use of columns in the cemetery conveys the same image. (FHC.)

Section 33. The temple style of marker was used to depict heaven. The temple marker shown here also contains an urn. This marker is for the Benjamin family. (FHC.)

Section 62. This view of family lots represents the styles of markers and headstone that became popular after World War I, replacing the Victorian styles. (FHC.)

Two

Milwaukee Beer Barons

Beer has greatly influenced Milwaukee's industry and culture since the mid-1800s. Milwaukee became the beer capital of America with names like Blatz, Gettelman, Miller, Pabst, and Schlitz, but the story of Milwaukee beer starts before these iconic barons of industry.

Good farmland, good water, and similarities to home drew masses of European emigrants, especially from Germany. The people of Germany brought their culture, their craftsmanship, and of course, their beer. Through hard work and generations of expertise, Milwaukee became a mecca for brewing.

For many years, Milwaukee breweries were the nation's top producers of beer, with Pabst and Schlitz taking turns as leader until the start of Prohibition in 1919. Prior to Prohibition, the breweries owned or contracted buildings called "tied houses," which sold only their product. This changed after Prohibition, when the practice became illegal.

Many of these buildings still stand with their brewery logo as a reminder of what they were prior to Prohibition. Milwaukee had approximately 30 breweries in 1860, most in the form of small self-brewing taverns. By 1880, only 15 were considered big businesses, and only six made it through the 13 years of Prohibition.

It is interesting to note that in the early 1900s, Milwaukee was half the size it is today but had twice the number of taverns and tied houses. Prohibition, two world wars, continued industrialization, and globalization brought turbulence and change. Through it all, beer remained an important and integral part of Milwaukee.

A list of beer barons residing at Forest Home Cemetery can be found on page 126. At least once a year, a tour visits many on the list.

—Robert L. Giese

Section 8. Jacob Best Sr. (1786–1861), with his four sons, established Milwaukee's largest brewery in 1844. By 1859, his son Phillip had become the sole proprietor, changing the name to the Phillip Best Brewing Company. Phillip's daughter Maria married Capt. Frederick Pabst in 1862, and Frederick became vice president in 1864. Meanwhile, the Melms southside brewery was established by C.T. Melms in 1853. After Melms passed away in 1869, his brewery was acquired by the Phillip Best Brewery. Eventually, Pabst took the helm, and on March 12, 1889, the name was officially changed to the Pabst Brewing Company. Its slogan became "He drinks Best who drinks Pabst." (FHC.)

Best Monument. After over 100 years without a monument, a fundraiser was held, and on May 22, 2011, there was a gathering for the unveiling of the Jacob Best Sr. monument. (LM.)

SECTION 40. Capt. Frederick Pabst (1836–1904) married Phillip Best's daughter Maria. Emil Schandein married Phillip's other daughter, Lisette. Emil Schandein (1840–1888) ran the Phillip Best Brewing Company until he passed away. Soon after, Frederick Pabst became the head of the brewery and changed the name to the Pabst Brewing Company. By the end of the 19th century, the Pabst Brewing Company was the largest producer of lager beer in America at over 1 million barrels annually. Pabst died on New Year's Day 1904. (FHC.)

PABST BEER AD. This is a Pabst ad from the 1893 World's Columbian Exposition, where Pabst was declared the best beer in America. (MCHS.)

Section 40. Pictured is the site of the Pabst and Emil Schandein family monument. The monument is all marble. (LM.)

Pabst Family Lot. Here is another view of the Pabst family burial site showing a row of six children who passed away at birth or a very young age. While the family had great success, they also had great sorrows. Notice the floral display on each grave. These were commonly called "grave blankets," and ground cover such as myrtle was used for the planting. It was also common to have a "winter blanket" of evergreens. (LM.)

Tied House. Pabst and other breweries had tied houses like this one in Milwaukee's Historic Third Ward. Tied houses were owned or rented by the breweries and only served their beer. This practice was outlawed after Prohibition. (Both, RLG.)

Section 25. Simon Reutelshofer established a new brewery in 1840. After years of ownership and location changes, C.T. Melms (1819–1869) became sole owner of the brewery by 1853 and named it the Menomonee Brewery. Melms died from tetanus in 1869. Twenty-one months later, the brewery was sold to the Phillip Best Brewing Company and renamed Best's South Side Brewery. (LM.)

Melms Monument. After 144 years without a monument, on August 18, 2013, the new Melms monument was dedicated. The rear of the monument has a year-by-year history of the brewery. (LM.)

Section 36. Joseph Schlitz (1831–1875) started as a bookkeeper for brewer August Krug, who owned Krug's Brewery. After Krug passed away, Schlitz married Krug's widow, Anna. He renamed the brewery the Joseph Schlitz Brewing Company, well-known as "The Beer That Made Milwaukee Famous." (FHC.)

Schlitz Brewery, Early 1900s. This picture of the brewery along Third Street was taken at the turn of the 20th century. At the time, Schlitz and Pabst vied for the number-one beer by volume, measured in barrels. (MCHS.)

SECTION 36. The Joseph Schlitz monument stands in Forest Home Cemetery. This monument is known as a cenotaph, a memorial for a person who is not buried at that location. The carved boat is a clue to the story. (LM.)

SCHLITZ CENOTAPH. On a visit to his home in Stuttgart, Germany, for a sharpshooting tournament in 1875, the ship Schlitz was on, the SS *Friedrich Schiller*, ran into rocks and sank. His body was never found. The ship is carved into the Schlitz monument. His wife and her nephews, the Uihleins, inherited the business. (LM.)

TIED HOUSE. Schlitz Brewery had tied house arrangements with over 1,000 saloons. This arrangement between bar and brewery was no longer allowed after Prohibition. (RLG.)

SECTION 37. The story of beer baron Valentin Blatz (1826–1894) started with Johann Braun, who built a small brewery on today's East Juneau Avenue known as City Brewery. After arriving in Milwaukee, Blatz worked for Braun and eventually opened his own brewery next door. After Braun passed away in 1851, Blatz married Braun's widow, Louisa, and united the two breweries, thus creating the noted Blatz Brewing Company, "Milwaukee's Finest Beer." (FHC.)

BEER AD. This Blatz ad from the early 1900s speaks for itself. (MCHS.)

Section 37. The massive granite Blatz family mausoleum is Wisconsin's largest and at the time of its construction (1901–1902) was considered the largest in the Midwest. Inside, in the middle area, Valentin and Louisa Blatz each have a sarcophagus, and family members' caskets are in pullout drawers on three walls; each drawer holds two caskets. Because of its size, family members can still use this mausoleum for interments. (LM.)

The Blatz Mausoleum. The Blatz family mausoleum has an urn above the door with music notes for handles. The family loved music and donated money for the community's enjoyment of music. The large bandshell in Washington Park was funded by the Blatz family. (LM.)

SECTION 33. Emil Czarnecki established the Milwaukee Independent Brewery. By 1920, Henry Bills Sr. (1868–1951) had become its president and treasurer. His son Henry Jr. became head brewmaster in 1933. The brewery was known for its Braumeister label. When Henry Sr. passed away, Braumeister produced 150,000 barrels a year for 19 states. After Henry Bills Sr. died, Harry Bills Jr. became president. (LM.)

SECTION 4. John Graf Sr. (1853–1930) went into partnership with Phillip H. Madlener in 1873. They produced Weiss (white) beer. By 1883, Graf had full control of the brewery. The family continued making beer and soda until Prohibition. After Prohibition, the company made only soda, including the well-known Grandpa Graf Root Beer. (LM.)

SECTION 33. Frederick "Fritz" Gettelman's (1887–1954) brewery was originally called the Menomonee Brewery. The Gettelman Brewery was started by George Schweichart. Gettelman's father, Adam, married Schweichart's daughter Magdelana. When Adam died, Fritz took over the brewery. Years later, the brewery was run by fourth-generation Gettelmans Fred and Tom. In 1961, it was sold to the Miller Brewing Company. (NG.)

BREWERY WORKERS. Gettleman Brewery workers are pictured on a break around 1887. Beer breaks were common in the beer industry in Milwaukee, and after Prohibition, some breweries allowed employees a case of beer per week as part of their employment. Notice that the name is spelled with two *n*'s instead of one. The employee at right in the first row appears to have a gun in his hand, or perhaps a tool of some type. (MCHS.)

SECTION 33. Franz Falk (1823–1882) and a partner acquired the Eagle Brewery in 1856. After the partnership ended, Falk opened the new Bavaria Brewery in 1871. After his death, his sons Frank and Louis took over the company, changing the name to Franz Falk Brewing Company. Later, the Jung and Borchert Breweries merged with the Falk Brewery. After two fires, the brewery was sold to the Pabst Brewing Company. At the time of the fire, it was regarded as one of the largest breweries in Milwaukee. Falk's son Herman used an abandoned shed for other ventures, which led to the formation of the renowned Falk Gear Company. (Left, PM; below, LM.)

Three

Milwaukee Mayors and Politicians

Most of Milwaukee's mayors are buried at Forest Home Cemetery, including two of the city founders and one of the three Socialist mayors. George Walker was the founder of the area today called Walker's Point. Byron Kilbourn established the west side of the Milwaukee River, which was called Kilbourn Town.

Terms of office for mayor started at one year, then increased to two years, and are currently four years. At the time of this printing, Milwaukee has had 41 mayors, 26 of whom are buried at Forest Home Cemetery and are recognized once every year on the Mayors Tour. Forest Home also has five governors and five US representatives residing in its grounds.

A list of all the mayors buried at Forest Home Cemetery can be found on page 127.

—Robert L. Giese

Chapel Section. Frank Zeidler (1912–2006) graduated from West Division High School (today Milwaukee School of the Arts) and attended Marquette University. He was the last of Milwaukee's three Socialist mayors. Prior to his election, he worked as a land surveyor and in the engineering department for the Milwaukee Road. Zeidler never drove a car. (Left, MCHS; below, LM.)

CHAPEL SECTION IN MEMORIAL. Carl F. Zeidler (1908–1942) graduated from Marquette University in 1931 and was briefly employed in Chicago. Once back in Milwaukee, he was appointed assistant city attorney in 1936. Zeidler was considered an extraordinary attorney with his overwhelming success in winning cases. He won his campaign for mayor against Socialist incumbent Daniel Hoan by 12,000 votes. At his inauguration, he was the youngest executive of any large American city, though Sherman Becker had been younger. In April 1942, Zeidler asked for a leave from his duties to join the US Naval Reserve. He was assigned to a merchant ship and asked for a commission and to be appointed to one of the most dangerous jobs. His ship, the USS *La Salle*, was torpedoed on November 7, 1942, off South Africa. No bodies were ever recovered. (Both, FHC.)

SECTION 33. Sherman M. Becker (1876–1949) was Milwaukee's youngest mayor at 29. He attracted nationwide attention for his youth. Prior to being mayor, he served on the county board and common council. He drove a red auto to New York with a banner on the side reading "Milwaukee Boy Mayor." During his trip, he stopped at Theodore Roosevelt's house at Sagamore Hill, Oyster Bay, New York. (FHC.)

SHERMAN BECKER. Mayor Becker did not like the sidewalk clocks on Milwaukee streets, including this one on Wisconsin Avenue, and had all of them torn down. Needless to say, this was a very controversial act by a mayor. (MCHS.)

SECTION 6. George Peck (1840–1916) was a newspaper publisher and founded newspapers in Ripon and Lacrosse, Wisconsin. In 1878, Peck moved his newspaper to Milwaukee, calling it *Peck's Sun*. He was elected mayor in 1890 and resigned when he was elected Wisconsin's governor, serving from 1891 to 1894. (FHC.)

GEORGE PECK. Peck was also known for his writings, including *Peck's Bad Boy*, which became the basis for several films and a short-lived television show. He died of Bright's Disease, a kidney disease. (FHC.)

HUNTING FOR THE BAD BOY.

PECK'S

BAD BOY

AND HIS PA.

BY GEO. W. PECK,

Author of "PECK'S FUN," "PECK'S SUNSHINE," and Editor "PECK'S SUN."

WITH ILLUSTRATIONS BY GEAN SMITH.

CHICAGO:
BELFORD, CLARKE & CO.
1883.

SECTION 33. John Koch (1841–1907) was born in Hamburg, Germany. He became a tanner in his father's shop. He received his party's nomination for lieutenant governor in 1892 but instead was elected mayor of Milwaukee in 1893. He served as mayor when city hall was built in 1895. The architect was Henry Koch (no relation). (Left, FHC; below, LM.)

City Hall Construction. This is a picture of Milwaukee City Hall during construction in 1894. (MCHS.)

City Hall Completed. City hall is seen here between 1905 and 1910. When completed in 1905, it was the third-tallest structure in the United States. The two taller structures were the Washington Monument and Philadelphia City Hall. (MCHS.)

William Lynde. William Pitt Lynde (1817–1885) was state attorney general, state senator, member of the US House of Representatives, and US district attorney. In 1842, he founded the law firm that is today Foley & Lardner. (FHC.)

Section 19. One of William Lynde's daughters, Clara, married Henry Bradley, and they had two sons, Lynde and Harry, who started the Allen Bradley Corporation, a major employer for generations. Today, the company is known as Rockwell International. (LM.)

Section 14. Thomas Hoyt Brown (1839–1908) was born on his parents' farm at Sixteenth Street and Fond du Lac Avenue in Milwaukee. After moving to Pennsylvania, attracted by oil, he returned to Milwaukee in 1866. Back in Milwaukee, he went into partnership in a carriage manufacturing company that started out on Wisconsin and Jefferson Streets. That site is now the location of the federal building. Brown served as alderman from 1877 to 1880 and president of the common council. He was elected mayor from 1880 to 1881 and again for a two-year term from 1888 to 1890. (Right, FHC; below, LM.)

Section 31. Hans Crocker (1815–1889) was born in Dublin, Ireland, and immigrated to America as a child. He studied law in Chicago and was active in Democratic politics. Later, he became a Republican during Abraham Lincoln's run for president. Crocker was a good friend of Byron Kilbourn and owned a lot of real estate in Kilbourntown. He helped Kilbourn promote the development of railroads in Wisconsin. He was chairman of a group that rewrote Milwaukee's city charter in 1851 and served a term as mayor in 1852. In addition, he was editor of Milwaukee's first newspaper, the *Milwaukee Advertiser.* In 1836, he was the private secretary to Henry Dodge, Wisconsin's first governor. (Left, FHC; below, LM.)

SECTION 31. George Walker (1811–1866) was one of three founders of Milwaukee. Today, the area he settled is called Walker's Point. Walker was a fur trader and eventually became a real estate promoter in Milwaukee. He was in the territorial legislature and was speaker of the house. He was twice voted Milwaukee's mayor. Walker built the first streetcar line in Milwaukee, which ran from St. Mary's Hospital to Walker's Point. He was also involved in the state's early railroads. He was successful in securing the location of the National Soldiers Home in Milwaukee. Today, Walker's Point is a very popular area, with bars and restaurants. (Right, FHC; below, LM.)

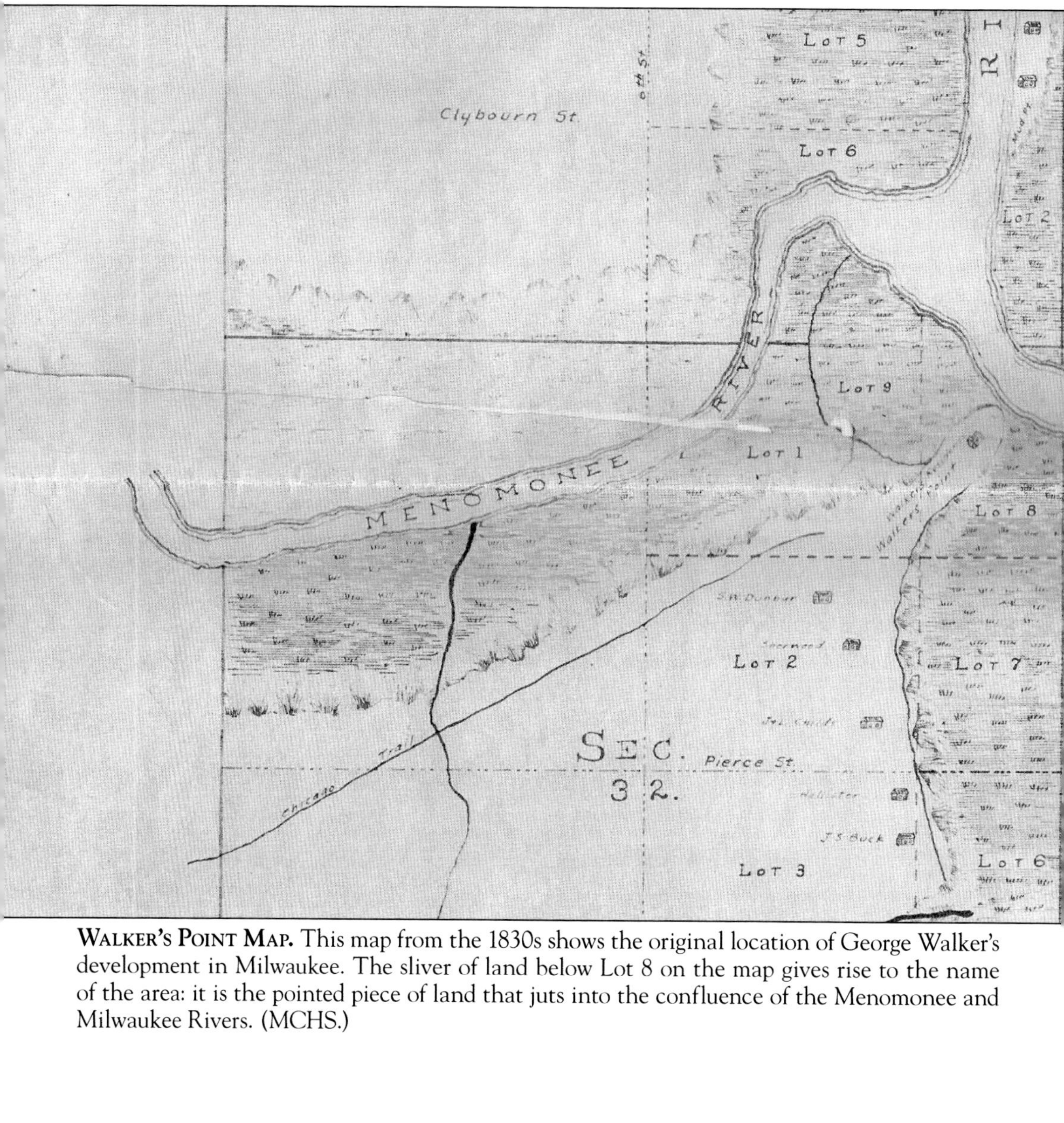

WALKER'S POINT MAP. This map from the 1830s shows the original location of George Walker's development in Milwaukee. The sliver of land below Lot 8 on the map gives rise to the name of the area: it is the pointed piece of land that juts into the confluence of the Menomonee and Milwaukee Rivers. (MCHS.)

Four

Famous Milwaukeeans

Describing someone as famous is relative to time and place. For this chapter, being buried at Forest Home Cemetery and having played a significant role in Milwaukee history serve as major criteria for selection.

Milwaukee is considered to have three founders: Solomon Juneau, Byron Kilbourn, and George Walker. Juneautown was on the east side of the Milwaukee River, Kilbourntown was on the west side of the river, and Walker's Point was on the south side. Walker and Kilbourn are buried at Forest Home and thus included here. Juneau is buried at Calvary Cemetery, on Milwaukee's near west side.

In 1836, Wisconsin became a US territory and was opened to land sales, speculators, and immigration. A prime requisite for developers was access to water, lake or river, and a safe harbor for Great Lakes schooners. Milwaukee fit these criteria with the best and largest harbor on the west side of Lake Michigan. The large harbor would be a boon to early commerce and would define the next 40 years of commerce.

Early settlers came to Milwaukee for opportunities to make money. Land speculators were buying and selling land, developers were building new buildings, commerce began, and the selling of goods and services grew quickly as the population grew. In 1836, Milwaukee was a small frontier town of 1,500; by 1850, the population zoomed to 20,000; and by the turn of the 20th century, it was 285,000. Population growth stimulated economic growth. Forest Home hosts the gravesites of industrialists, railroad magnates, bankers, innovative engineers, lumber barons, and people whose contributions helped Milwaukee to grow.

This chapter will review just some of these many people and their contributions, but it is not inclusive of all the historical Milwaukee figures at rest at Forest Home Cemetery. As Milwaukee historian John Gurda said, "What lies beneath the trees at Forest Home is the foundation of Milwaukee."

—Paul A. Haubrich

Section 32. Alexander Mitchell (1817–1887) was born in Scotland, immigrated to Chicago, and in 1838 came to Milwaukee, where he started the Marine Insurance Company. In practice, this was a bank and not an insurance company. He used the term "insurance" because banks had a poor reputation in the 1830s. His banking skills led to other investments, such as the Chicago, Milwaukee & St. Paul Railroad, which became the largest railroad to serve the upper Midwest and northwestern United States. His interests also expanded to insurance and property investments associated with the railroad. He was considered one of Wisconsin's first millionaires. His office building still stands at the southeast corner of Michigan and Water Streets downtown. (FHC.)

The Mitchell Family. The Mitchell monument is located on a slightly elevated rise. The monument uses the sarcophagus style with columns at the corners. The columns were used to signify entry into heaven in Victorian symbolism. Note that behind and to the left are statues of two boys playing. These are two of Mitchell's children, Georgie and Willie, who died early in childhood. It should be noted that his wife, Martha, is not buried at this site. She died in Florida and was buried there. (FHC.)

SECTION 32. Gen. Billy Mitchell (1879–1936) was the grandson of Alexander Mitchell and was raised in the Mitchell home on the south side of Milwaukee. He was a West Point graduate and attained the rank of general by the First World War. He is considered the father of American air power, becoming a strong advocate of the use of planes in wartime. (FHC.)

GEN. BILLY MITCHELL. Milwaukee's airport was originally named General Billy Mitchell Field. The airport changed its name in 2018 to Mitchell Field, dropping the longer title. Mitchell's push for the use of airplanes for military purposes put him at loggerheads with other Army generals who lacked his foresight. Mitchell is credited with the start of the Army Air Corps. (FHC.)

SECTION 9. Frederick Layton (1827–1891), born in Little Wilbraham, England, immigrated to Milwaukee in 1848. John, his father, was trained as a butcher in England, and Frederick and his son began a butcher and slaughtering operation on West Water Street in Milwaukee. Their business prospered, and they partnered with John Plankinton to expand the slaughtering operation in the Menomonee Valley. This partnership with Plankinton ended, and the Laytons formed their own operation. Plankinton partnered with another Milwaukee family to create the Plankinton and Armour meat packing company. (FHC.)

FREDERICK LAYTON. Layton was also an art collector, and in 1885, he built the Layton School of Art and Design, which became Milwaukee's first art museum. The Layton art collection became the foundation for today's Milwaukee Art Museum. (FHC.)

SECTION 19. Daniel Newhall (1821–1895) was a merchant, investor, and land speculator who became a wealthy grain dealer as Milwaukee became a significant factor in the wheat and grain industry. The market for grains developed rapidly during the Civil War, as the Mississippi River was blockaded at New Orleans. This meant that the only viable port for shipping was Milwaukee with its deep harbor. The grain was shipped by rail to Milwaukee, loaded onto boats, and shipped to the Buffalo area. It was then offloaded to barges on the Erie Canal and thus down the Hudson and to the world. (FHC.)

DANIEL NEWHALL. Newhall built the Newhall House hotel in the late 1850s but later sold it. In February 1883, the hotel had a disastrous fire in which 69 people perished. The majority of the bodies could not be identified, so a mass grave was created at Forest Home with a special monument. Newhall always regretted giving his name to the hotel, as many associated him with the fire. (FHC.)

Section 10. Christopher Sholes (1819–1890) and Carlos Glidden are credited with developing the first operational typewriter. Sholes was a newspaper man and had a strong interest in trying to develop a machine that could produce type like those used by typesetters in the newspaper industry. Sholes's initial attempts were not successful, but his progress was noted and was of interest to others. (FHC.)

Sholes, Glidden and Soule Machine—Patent of July 14, 1868.

Sholes Typewriter. One of Sholes's issues was to arrange the keys so that when pressed they did not bind or interfere with the next key strike. One of his solutions was to create a unique key arrangement that led to what today is called the QWERTY keyboard. When school children take tours and Sholes's invention is mentioned, they have no idea what a typewriter is, but they know the QWERTY keyboard. (FHC.)

SECTION 24. Byron Kilbourn (1801–1870) is considered one of the three founders of Milwaukee. He was a land speculator who bought large tracts on the west side of the Milwaukee River in 1836, when Wisconsin became a US territory. In addition, he is credited with founding Wisconsin Dells, originally called Kilbourntown, and West Bend. Kilbourn was a speculator in many adventures in early Milwaukee, including a canal to the Mississippi River, early railroads, and other land deals. Kilbourn left Milwaukee after the Civil War and went to the next land boom in Florida. (FHC.)

KILBOURN FAMILY. Kilbourn passed away in 1870 and was buried in Florida. His wife and daughter preceded him in death and were buried on the Kilbourn lot at Forest Home. Kilbourn had been one of the 50 prominent Milwaukeeans to buy early lots at the cemetery. In 1998, a group of historically minded citizens raised money to return Kilbourn from Florida to Milwaukee and bury him with his wife and daughter. (FHC.)

SECTION 24. On the back side of Kilbourn's monument is the story of his return to Milwaukee. At the dedication of this monument, former Wisconsin governor Lee Sherman Dreyfus concluded his remarks: "Tonight I can go home and tell my wife Joyce that Byron Kilbourn is now sleeping with his wife in Milwaukee and not with his mistress in Florida." (FHC.)

INCREASE LAPHAM. To the left and four graves back of Kilbourn's monument is the grave of Increase Lapham, who worked for Kilbourn upon his arrival in Milwaukee as a surveyor. Lapham was a man of many skills. He is considered Wisconsin' first naturalist, and his records of weather data helped develop the US Weather Bureau, of which he is sometimes considered one of the founders. (FHC.)

SECTION 27. Edward Holton (1815–1892) was active in a number of Milwaukee businesses involving banking, insurance, land speculation, and railroads. He was also active in a variety of abolitionist movements, including forming the Wisconsin Liberty Party, a political party against slavery. In 1854, he and others were involved in creating the Republican Party, which chose Abraham Lincoln as its presidential candidate in 1860. (FHC.)

EDWARD HOLTON. Holton sponsored a group of Milwaukeeans to settle in Kansas so they could vote against the new state becoming a slave state. The town of Holton, Kansas, is named after him. (FHC.)

SECTION 19. John Plankinton (1820–1891) was a businessman, stockyard owner, and owner of the Plankinton Hotel. Over the years, he would partner with other Milwaukeeans in the stockyard and slaughter house business. Layton, Armour, and Cudahy, all names in the industry, worked with Plankinton. Cudahy meat packing of Cudahy, Wisconsin, is still in business today. (FHC.)

PLANKINTON STATUE. Plankinton built the Plankinton Hotel in 1867. It was considered the finest hotel in Wisconsin. The hotel remained in business until 1921, when it was torn down by John's family to build the Plankinton Arcade, a business and entertainment hub in downtown Milwaukee. It is currently called the Grand Avenue. A statue of Plankinton still stands in the middle of the arcade. (FHC.)

SECTION LAWN PLACE. Samuel Marshall (1820–1907) founded a private bank called the Samuel Marshall Company in 1847 with an initial focus on loans to local businesses. In 1852, he was joined by a new business partner, Charles Ilsley, and the bank became known as Marshall and Ilsley Bank, or as locals called it, M&I. Marshall was active in Milwaukee business circles and served on the board of Northwestern Mutual Insurance Company for many years. He also founded the Bank of Madison in 1853 and served as its president until 1889. (FHC.)

CHARLES ILSLEY. Charles F. Ilsley (1827–1904) joined Marshall in 1852, and the bank prospered by focusing on local business loans and conservative business practices. The bank was formally incorporated in 1888 under new state laws. In the financial crisis of 2008, Marshall and Ilsley Bank was sold to BMO Harris Bank of Chicago, and today operates as BMO Harris Bank in Wisconsin. (FHC.)

Section 32. Harrison Ludington (1812–1891) was an entrepreneur, politician, and active citizen. Shortly after arriving in Milwaukee, Ludington built one of the first office buildings in the city. He was active in the land and lumber businesses; his first venture, with his brother, was a lumber operation in Columbus, Wisconsin. They also had a lumber operation in northern Wisconsin called the Tomahawk Land and Lumber Company, along with lumber interests in Michigan and Louisiana. (FHC.)

Harrison Ludington. Ludington was active in politics, serving as mayor of Milwaukee. In 1876, he was elected governor of Wisconsin. The Ludington lot at Forest Home is the largest family lot, with 50 graves. Three families—Ludington, Patton, and Van Schiek—share this lot. They are all related by marriage. Notice the pillow-style headstones used for individual markers and that not all family members have individual markers. (FHC.)

SECTION 33. George Brumder (1839–1910) started a small publishing house for religious books in German. The business grew into a large publishing house for German newspapers, magazines, and books. It was considered the largest German publisher in the United States. It all came to an abrupt end with the start of World War I, and the office building known as the Germania Building was renamed the Brumder Building. It is still in use in downtown Milwaukee. (FHC.)

BRUMDER FAMILY LOT. The Brumder monument is a variant of an obelisk with a rounded base instead of a square base. This is a good example of a family lot, with many generations buried and memorialized at this location. Many of the lots in this section of the cemetery are larger family lots, a common practice in the late 1800s. (FHC.)

SECTION D. William T. Green (1860–1911), Milwaukee's first African American lawyer and a civil rights activist, was born in Ontario, Canada, just north of Niagara Falls, in May 1860. He was educated in Canada, attending St. Catherine's College prior to immigration to Wisconsin in 1887. His first job was as a janitor in the state capitol. He was able to enroll in the University of Wisconsin Law School and was one of the few African American graduates, completing his degree in 1892. Green was instrumental through his legal practice in getting the Wisconsin Civil Rights Act of 1893 enacted, prohibiting racial discrimination in public facilities. (FHC.)

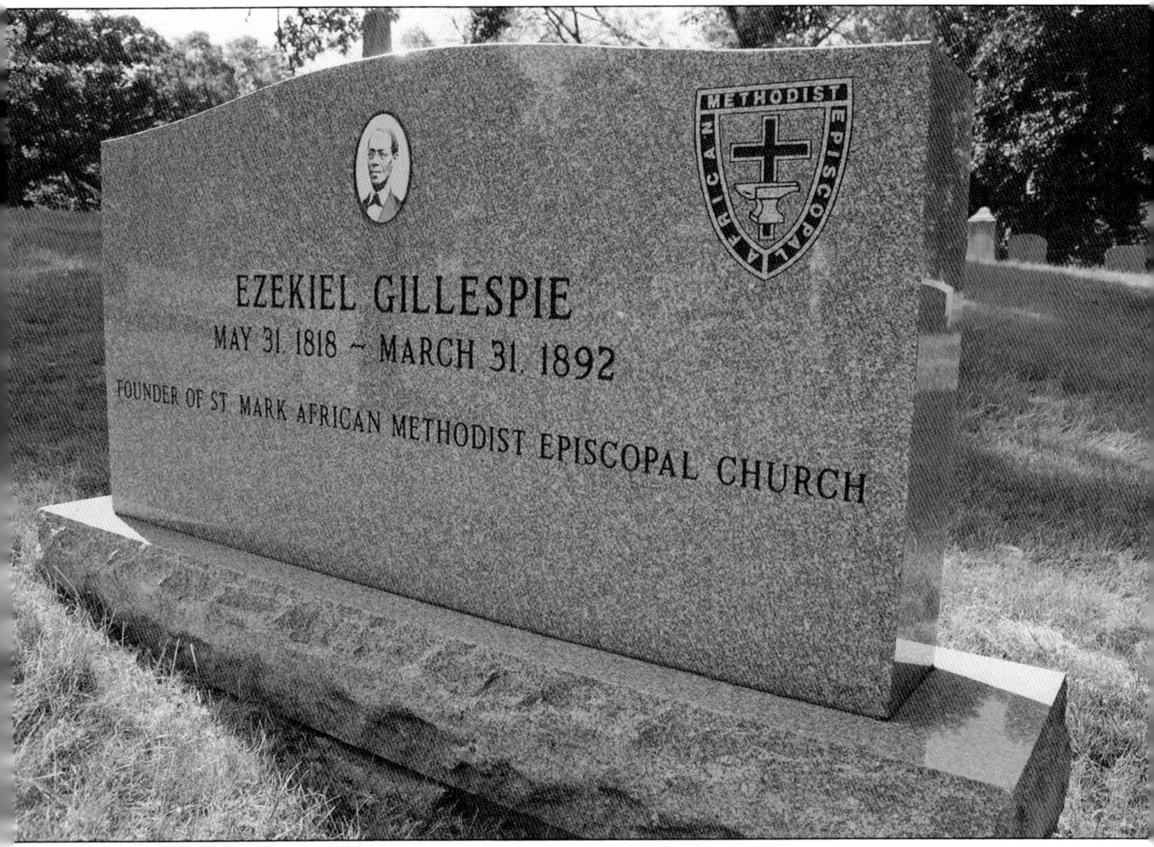

SECTION 31. Ezekiel Gillespie (1818–1892), born in Green County, Tennessee, bought his freedom for $800 and moved first to Indiana and then Milwaukee. He sold groceries and worked for the railroad. Gillespie was instrumental in winning a court case over being denied the right to vote. In 1866, the Wisconsin Supreme Court ruled in his favor, thus giving all African American men the right to vote in Wisconsin for the first time. He was the founder of the first African American church in Milwaukee. His gravestone, a new one donated by St. Mark African Methodist Episcopal Church, honors his efforts. (FHC.)

SECTION 33. Alfred Lunt and his wife, Lynn Fontanne, were famous stage actors in both the United States and England. Both are buried on the left of the row of family members. Their monument bears the name A.D. Lunt. This marker is for a family lot that belongs to Alfred Lunt's father, also named Alfred. (FHC.)

TEN CHIMNEYS. Alfred Lunt and Lynn Fontanne had a summer home in Genesse Depot, Wisconsin, and entertained famous actors and personalities there from the 1920s to the 1960s. Today, this home is called Ten Chimneys and is listed in the National Register of Historic Places; it is open to visitors. (FHC.)

Five

Industrial Milwaukee

The end of the Civil War marked the beginning of a new era for Milwaukee. It was no longer a new frontier town but a growing city of 70,000 plus, and new innovators arrived on the scene. Milwaukee was in the vanguard of industries expanding the power of the steam engine to develop new ways to increase efficiency and productivity.

Central to both manufacturing and innovation was the E.P. Allis Company, a local machine shop that expanded from less than 100 employees to 15,000 within 30 years. In the 1870s and 1880s, Allis developed steam engines, lumber milling equipment, and flour milling equipment, all of which brought big changes to those industries. Allis Corporation continued to expand into steam-generated electricity, hydroelectric generators, agricultural equipment, and many other areas in the following decades until closing in 1984.

One of the defining elements of Milwaukee industry was its machine shop skills. The city's machinists developed equipment for the mining industry, including excavators, stone crushers, mine lifts, and in the modern era, large earth-moving equipment. Harnischfeger Corporation developed overhead cranes for manufacturing facilities. Nordberg developed diesel engines for the US Navy. Vilter Corporation developed commercial refrigeration. A man named Davidson, with others, developed a motorized bike.

Innovation was also the name of the game at A.O. Smith Company, which took its bike frame technology and become one of the largest makers of automobile frames in the United States, producing at its peak 10,000 frames a week. A.O. Smith became an innovator of the glass-lined hot-water tank as well as the largest maker of bomb casings during World War II.

Not to be outdone was Thomas L. Smith, who had worked for Allis Corporation as well as other machine shops. He developed the idea of a portable cement mixer that would become essential to the construction industry. His first mixer was on a horse-drawn wagon with a steam engine to rotate the drum.

—Paul A. Haubrich

SECTION 36. The Allis mausoleum is the second largest of the eight mausoleums at Forest Home. Edward P. Allis and his wife, Margaret, are interred in two sarcophagi in the center with 24 additional spaces inside the mausoleum. There are another 24 spaces around the mausoleum for traditional burial. In recent years, family members have chosen to be buried outside rather than inside the mausoleum. The mausoleum is on a rise above a small lake. (LM.)

EDWARD PHELPS ALLIS. Edward Phelps Allis (1824–1889) was not an engineer but a good business manager. He attributed much of his success to hiring the best engineers and letting them innovate. His early success was in steam, flour milling, and lumber milling equipment. (FHC.)

ALLIS MACHINE SHOP. Edwin Phelps Allis Company's early plant was in Milwaukee's Third Ward. Allis bought this machine shop in 1860 after having sold out his share of a tannery in Two Rivers, Wisconsin. His first big break was winning the contract to develop the first municipal water system for the city of Milwaukee. His success with the project led to installing other water systems in the Midwest. (FHC.)

ALLIS COMPANY. As the company grew, Allis moved his plant to a 125-acre facility in what is now West Allis, Wisconsin. This plant at its peak employed 15,000 people, and generations of Milwaukeeans worked at the company that became Allis Chalmers Corporation in 1908. At times, it was considered the largest machine shop in the world. (FHC.)

SECTION 33. Bruno Nordberg (1858–1924), a Finnish engineer who originally worked at E.P. Allis, left to form his own company, Nordberg Manufacturing Corporation. Like Allis, he specialized in steam, focusing on smaller, more efficient engines. (FHC.)

ORIGINAL THIRD WARD PLANT. Nordberg's original plant, like so many other early industrialists, was in the Third Ward in Milwaukee. Nordberg eventually moved to a larger facility farther south and remained in business until the 1980s. Nordberg Manufacturing developed a specialty in larger diesel engines, with the US Navy as its primary customer for decades. The company also developed specialties in mining and rock-crushing machinery. (FHC.)

SECTION 9. Henry Harnischfeger (1855–1920), a German immigrant, came to Milwaukee in 1882 and entered into business with Adolphus Pawling, who owned a small machine shop in the Third Ward. It was primarily a job shop serving larger companies like the Allis Corporation. Its big break was the opportunity to repair and improve an overhead crane for the E.P. Allis Corporation. This led to the development of the Harnischfeger overhead crane, used by many companies. They reportedly sold over 11,000 cranes. (FHC.)

ALONZO PAWLING. Alonzo Pawling (1857–1914) was the original business partner with Henry Harnischfeger when they began their Pawling and Harnischfeger machine shop in Milwaukee's Third Ward. One of their early successes was the overhead cranes used in large industrial plants. They established the corporate symbol of P&H in 1884, which is still in use today, having been used on hundreds of thousands of pieces of equipment over the past 135 years. Today, the company is owned by the Komatsu Corporation. (FHC.)

SECTION 33. A.O. Smith (1859–1913) started in the bicycle business with his father, who developed a method of producing a stronger frame by a special bending process. A.O. Smith realized that early auto frames were not structurally sound, so he took the tube-bending idea from the bike frame and applied it to the auto business, with Cadillac as his first customer. Henry Ford started ordering large numbers of frames, reaching 10,000 a week. (FHC.)

A.O. SMITH CORPORATION. A.O. Smith developed other products over the years, including the first glass-lined hot-water heater, today's standard. During World War II, A.O. Smith Corporation had a number of government contracts and was the largest manufacturer of bomb casings. (FHC.)

SECTION 33. Guido Pfister (1818–1891), born in Germany, owned a leather goods store on West Water Street in Milwaukee in the 1840s. His cousin Frederick Vogel arrived in Milwaukee in 1851, and together they formed Pfister and Vogel Tanning Company. Their tannery became the largest in the United States by 1910. The presence of a tanning industry also fostered a large leather goods industry in Milwaukee, primarily shoes. (FHC.)

PFISTER FAMILY. Pfister's monument is a large version of a sarcophagus style with a woman in mourning atop the monument. She has a reverent gaze and very stylized hair. Just before his death, Guido Pfister and his family began construction of the Pfister Hotel on the corner of Wisconsin Avenue and Jefferson Street. It is considered the premier hotel in Milwaukee and is still in operation 125 years later. (FHC.)

SECTION 36. Frederick Vogel Sr. (1823–1892) was born in Germany and trained in the leather tanning industry. His arrival in Milwaukee in 1851 allowed him to apply his trade in the new Pfister and Vogel Tannery. One necessary element for the tanning business in the 1850s was access to trees for tannin. The bark was soaked in vats to create a brine that was used to begin the processing of cowhides into usable leather. (FHC.)

VOGEL MONUMENT. The Vogel monument is in the sarcophagus style, using wreath ornamentation that signifies the victory over death. Vogel, like many others in this chapter, is located in Section 36. This and nearby Section 33 hold many of the business leaders of the late 19th and early 20th centuries. (FHC.)

Section 38. William A. Davidson (1870–1937) was one of the famous Davidson brothers who, along with William Harley, developed the iconic Harley-Davidson motorcycle. Harley and two of William's brothers formed the company in 1903. The Harley-Davidson story is one of classic American ingenuity in developing a new product that would capture people's imagination. (FHC.)

Davidson Family. The Davidson lot has a marker that is sometimes referred to as a shield. It provides the backdrop for a family name that suggests success. When Harley-Davidson Corporation holds one of its anniversary biker fests to commemorate its founding, Harley riders come to the cemetery to pay homage to the Davidson family. (FHC.)

SECTION 33. Thomas L. Smith (1855–1921), founder of the T.L. Smith Company, was a Massachusetts Institute of Technology engineering graduate who worked for E.P. Allis, Harnischfeger, and Nordberg before forming his own engineering company. One of his major innovations was the development of the portable cement mixer. A small steam engine ran a tumbler device that allowed cement to be mixed mechanically in large quantities at a job location. The first cement mixer was mounted on a horse-drawn wagon. Milwaukee became the center of cement mixer manufacturing until the Second World War. (FHC.)

T.L. SMITH. The T.L Smith Corporation, like many of the other industrial enterprises in this chapter, moved into the mining business, specializing in rock-crushing equipment. The Smith family monument is in Section 33, where many industrialists from the late 1800s are located. These industrialists gave Milwaukee the nickname "Machine Shop to the World." (FHC.)

Six

Historic Women

The accomplishments, lives, and stories of women buried at Forest Home Cemetery from the founding of Milwaukee to modern times are often untold and overlooked in history books. The simple markers and sometimes unmarked graves of the women bear no indication of the significant contributions they made to the development of the city, state, and nation. However, the women of Forest Home Cemetery are not to be forgotten.

Often, women worked through groups or their churches to enact social change. Milwaukee's Children's Hospital was founded in 1894 in a home on Brady Street by seven women, five of whom are buried at Forest Home Cemetery. The first Milwaukee Soldiers Home was started in 1864 by the women of the West Side Soldiers Aid Society, many of whom are buried at the cemetery. Wisconsin's first woman's club, designed to educate and enrich the lives of Milwaukee women, was chartered in 1876 by a group of 18 women, 14 of whom are buried at the cemetery.

There were many historical firsts for the women of Forest Home Cemetery. These include Mathilde Anneke, the first editor of a Milwaukee women's newspaper in 1852; Dr. Laura Wolcott, Wisconsin's first female physician in 1857; Elizabeth Plankinton, patroness of Milwaukee's first public statue in 1885; Kate Pier Macintosh, the first female lawyer to argue a case before the Wisconsin Supreme Court in 1891; Mary Ellen Merrill, the first woman appointed Milwaukee school commissioner in 1895; Marion Ogden, Wisconsin's first juvenile probation officer in 1901; Alice Chester, founder of the Girl Scouts of Wisconsin in 1921; Mabel Watson Raimey, Wisconsin's first female African American lawyer in 1927; and Dickey Chapelle, the first female war photojournalist, killed in Vietnam in 1965.

In addition to being wives, mothers, and daughters, the women from Milwaukee's past were artists, authors, abolitionists, educators, doctors, founders of hospitals and orphan asylums, lawyers, leaders, philanthropists, suffragists, and more. Those highlighted in this chapter are just a few of the many truly wonderful stories of the women of Forest Home Cemetery.

—Anita M. Pietrykowski

Section 16. Susanna Custelo Watson (1798–1883) was a free black woman, seamstress, mother of five children, and the wife of Sully Watson, a freed slave from Virginia. Arriving in Milwaukee around 1850 to join their adult children and families already living here, the Watsons were among Milwaukee's earliest African American families. Fifteen family members of Sully and Susanna Watson are buried at Forest Home Cemetery. (AMP.)

Susanna Watson. Photographs of Susanna Watson and family came to light from the last known descendant, great-granddaughter Mabel Watson Raimey, who is buried in Section 45. Discovered in an old cardboard box in an antique store, the Watson family memorabilia was acquired by the Milwaukee Public Museum. Visitors will find information and a depiction of the Watson home in the museum's exhibit Streets of Old Milwaukee. (MPM.)

SECTION 15. Born in Lerchenhausen, Westphalia (Germany), and arriving in Milwaukee around 1850, Mathilde Franziska Anneke (1817–1884) was an outspoken advocate of equal rights for women and one of Milwaukee's leading suffragists. In 1852, she developed the first German-language newspaper that focused on women's issues, the *German Women's Times*. In 1865, she founded the Milwaukee Toechter-Institut, a school for girls. She devoted her life to teaching, writing, and lecturing on many reform topics. (MCHS.)

SECTION 36. Beer baroness Anna Maria Hartig Krug Schlitz (1819–1887) was twice the widow of a Milwaukee beer baron. Her first husband, August Krug (Section 8), died seven years after his brewery opened in Milwaukee. She married the brewery's bookkeeper, Joseph Schlitz, in 1858, but in 1875, he was lost at sea in a shipwreck off the coast of England. When she died in 1887, complete ownership of the Schlitz brewery went to August Krug's nephews, the Uihlein brothers. (MCHS.)

SECTION 10. Arriving in Milwaukee in 1857 after graduating from the Woman's Medical College of Pennsylvania, Dr. Laura Ross Wolcott (1826–1915) was Wisconsin's first female physician. During her career, she practiced at St. Mary's Hospital, the Protestant Orphan Asylum, and the Industrial School for Girls. Dr. Wolcott was also a suffragist, sponsoring Milwaukee's first suffrage convention in 1869. She served as the first president of the Wisconsin Woman Suffrage Association for 12 years. (MCHS.)

SECTION 36. Before women were allowed to vote, Mary Ellen Freeman Merrill (1831–1927) was appointed the first woman Milwaukee school commissioner in 1895. She is credited with requiring that public schools fly the American flag at their main entrances. She was a charter member of the Woman's Club of Wisconsin, the Wisconsin Humane Society, the Wisconsin Chapter of Colonial Dames, and Calvary Presbyterian Church. (AMP.)

SECTION 19. An artist by profession, Lydia Docenia Ely (1833–1914) is remembered as one of three key women in the establishment of the Soldiers Home in Milwaukee in 1869. Between 1896 and 1898, she collected over 2,800 autographs from noted Americans and compiled them into a gigantic autograph book. Weighing 50 pounds, it is now in the collection of the Milwaukee Central Public Library. (Wisconsin Historical Society, WHS-115853.)

***THE VICTORIOUS CHARGE*.** Because of her leadership and efforts to raise $30,000, Lydia Ely is considered the patroness of *The Victorious Charge*, a monument honoring Civil War soldiers in downtown Milwaukee. Thousands of visitors celebrated its dedication as Ely unveiled the monument, sculpted by John Severino Conway, on June 28, 1898. In 2016, she was recognized posthumously by the Museum of Wisconsin Art as a "true pioneer in the state's visual arts." (MCHS.)

SECTION 45. Bulah (or Beulah) Tobey Brinton (1835–1928) created Milwaukee's first community center in her Bay View neighborhood home. She offered classes in sewing, cooking, and English to the neighborhood's newly arrived immigrant iron mill workers. In addition to authoring two novels about the Civil War, she developed a free library in her home with more than 300 volumes. A park, street, and community center have all been named for Brinton in the neighborhood's past. (MCHS.)

THE BEULAH BRINTON HOUSE. Brinton's original home on South Superior Street is the current site of the Bay View Historical Society. In addition, the Beulah T. Brinton Community Center on South Bay Street, operated by the Recreation Division of Milwaukee Public Schools, continues to offer classes and recreational opportunities to Milwaukee residents. (AMP.)

SECTION 10. Georgia Green Stebbins (1846–1921) was the keeper of Milwaukee's North Point Lighthouse on the bluff overlooking Lake Michigan for 33 years. Arriving in Milwaukee in 1874, she found her father, Daniel Green (1804–1887), who was the lighthouse's keeper, in ill health. She unofficially performed his responsibilities for seven years before being appointed to the position herself. Her tenure as the lighthouse keeper ended when she retired in 1907. (AMP.)

NORTH POINT LIGHTHOUSE. Every four hours from sunset to sunrise, Georgia Green Stebbins ensured that the lamps were filled with oil, that the lenses were clean, and that the mechanism that operated the flash at the lighthouse was functioning. She recorded the passage of ships and the weather. She maintained the lighthouse's interior and grounds all while caring for her family. Her work is remembered in an exhibit at the North Point Lighthouse and Museum. (MCHS.)

SUSAN STUART FRACKELTON. Milwaukee native Susan Stuart Frackelton (1848–1932) was a well-known and recognized ceramics artist. Her ceramics and original china painting techniques won international acclaim, including nine awards at the 1893 Chicago World's Fair. Frackelton wrote the book *Tried by Fire* in 1885, which explained and illustrated her techniques for painting on ceramics. She invented a portable gas kiln that allowed women to make pottery in their own homes. (Wisconsin Historical Society, WHS-8857.)

SECTION 10. Frackelton created a magnificent illuminated manuscript, *Voices of Friends Concerning John Plankinton Milwaukee's Foremost Citizen, the Father of the West Side*. It was commissioned by Milwaukee's Elizabeth Ann Plankinton to honor her father. Frackelton's daughter, Gladys Frackelton Seely (1886–1973), hand-lettered all of the wording within. This priceless book is housed in the Richard and Lucile Krug Rare Books Collection at the Milwaukee Central Public Library. (AMP.)

SECTION 37. Born in Pachwaukee, Wisconsin, Harriet L. Barker Cramer (1848–1922) had a 54-year newspaper career. After coming to Milwaukee in 1864, she was hired by the *Evening Wisconsin* as a typesetter and proofreader. In 1869, she married the newspaper's editor, William E. Cramer (1817–1905), who was blind, deaf, and 30 years her senior. (MCHS.)

THE CRAMERS. Harriet Cramer and her husband were residents of the Newhall House Hotel in downtown Milwaukee when it caught fire on January 10, 1883. In order to escape, Harriet carried William through the burning and smoke-filled hallways to safety. After her husband passed away in 1905, Cramer became the president of the *Evening Wisconsin*, and ran the newspaper until 1918. She was a benefactress of Marquette University in Milwaukee, and Cramer Hall on the campus is named for her. (AMP.)

SECTION 27. Elizabeth Ann Plankinton (1853–1923) was called Milwaukee's municipal patroness because of her generosity. She donated $100,000 to build Milwaukee's first Young Women's Christian Association home for working women in 1899. Plankinton commissioned Milwaukee artist Susan Stuart Frackelton to create *The Voices of Friends Concerning John Plankinton* to honor her father's legacy. (MCHS.)

GEORGE WASHINGTON. Elizabeth Ann Plankinton donated the first public statue to the city, unveiled in 1885. Plankinton commissioned Richard Henry Park to create the bronze statue of George Washington. It was her idea to add the figure of the woman and the child at the base of the monument. The monument still stands on Ninth Street and Wisconsin Avenue. (MCHS.)

Section 36. Emelie Vogel Nunnemacher (1856–1949) was a benefactress in the development of the Milwaukee Children's Hospital. She began her involvement in 1894 and remained involved for the next 54 years. In 1915, she donated her fabulous mansion on Wisconsin Avenue so that a new children's hospital could be built there. Children's Hospital of Wisconsin annually recognizes a donor who demonstrates the same spirit of philanthropy with the Nunnemacher Award. (AMP.)

Section 4, Unmarked Grave. Lutie E. Stearns (1866–1943) helped to establish more than 150 free libraries, 1,400 traveling libraries, and 14 county library systems. She was instrumental in getting the state legislature to create the Wisconsin Free Library Commission in 1895. She also was an international lecturer on women's rights and wrote a column for the *Milwaukee Sentinel* called "As a Woman Sees It." In 2008, she was inducted into the Wisconsin Library Hall of Fame. (MCHS.)

Meta Schlichting Berger. Meta Schlichting Berger (1873–1944) was active in education, socialism, and women's suffrage. She served on the Milwaukee Board of School Directors for 30 years and was the first female president of the board, from 1915 to 1916. Berger was also a University of Wisconsin regent. She is one of 15 Wisconsin women whose names are inscribed on a plaque in the Washington office of the League of Women Voters in honor of their work for women's suffrage. (MCHS.)

Section 25. In 1944, Meta Schlichting Berger was buried at Forest Home Cemetery with no marker, even though her husband, Victor Berger (1860–1929), had a marker denoting his burial site. After attending a women's tour at the cemetery, Girl Scout Troop 8617 raised funds for nearly two years to purchase and donate a marker for Meta Berger. It was dedicated on June 24, 2017. (AMP.)

Section 34, Unmarked Grave. Lenore Harrison Cawker (1873–1932) led a life devoted to the relief of suffering animals. She was appalled at the way dogs were being euthanized at the city pound. She set aside her career as an artist, and from 1906 to 1930, she turned her home into Milwaukee's first animal shelter, called the Cawker Animal House. She used her personal inheritance for the care of thousands of cats, dogs, birds, and horses. (Wisconsin Historical Society, WHS-57391.)

Cawker Fountain. In 1914, Lenore Cawker donated a granite drinking fountain to the residents of Cawker City, Kansas, in memory of her father, Col. Emanuel Harrison Cawker (1848–1893), who founded the town in 1870. Designed to be a watering trough for horses, Lenore ensured that space for a water bowl was installed on each side for dogs and cats. A plaque on the fountain states, "A Merciful Man Is Merciful to His Beast." (Cawker City Museum.)

Marion G. Ogden. After graduating from a New York college, Milwaukee native Marion G. Ogden (1875–1976) was hired by the Boys' Club of Milwaukee to assist boys in the county jail. She volunteered to be Wisconsin's first juvenile parole officer in 1901 and was a strong advocate for a juvenile justice system in the state. She later served on the board of the Boys' Club for more than 40 years. (MCHS.)

Section 27. In 1935, Ogden was a founding member of the Milwaukee County Historical Society, and she wrote numerous articles for its monthly publications. In 1946, she wrote the book *Homes of Old Spring Street*, which featured the grand mansions and stories of Milwaukeeans who lived on what is now known as Wisconsin Avenue. She lived to be 101 years old. (AMP.)

Section 33. Alice Miller Chester (1893–1972) is best remembered for her involvement with the Girl Scouts, which spanned more than 50 years. She was the founder and the first president of the Girl Scouts of Milwaukee in 1921. Starting in 1928, she served as the national vice president of Girl Scouts while Herbert Hoover's wife, Lou Hoover, served as the national president. In 1970, she received an honorary doctorate from Lawrence University. (GSWS.)

Girl Scout Tours. Alice Miller Chester led fundraising efforts to purchase a 100-acre site on Booth Lake near East Troy, Wisconsin, for the Girl Scouts. Opening in 1924, it was named Camp Alice Chester in her honor. As a part of a tour offered to Girl Scouts at Forest Home Cemetery, Scouts visit the grave of Alice Chester and learn about her life and accomplishments. The Scouts do a grave rubbing to take back for their troop meetings. (AMP.)

SECTION 36 CENOTAPH. Author, lecturer, and Milwaukee television and radio personality Gertrude M. Puelicher (1894–1993) was an English teacher at Riverside High School early in her career. In the 1940s, she began writing the monthly column "God's Corner" for *Exclusively Yours* magazine. She wrote more than 500 before her death, and her monthly column is still published in the magazine. She hosted the weekly television program *The Other 98*, which featured the positive contributions of teenagers. (AMP.)

SECTION B. Ardie Clark Halyard (1896–1989) cofounded Columbia Savings and Loan in Milwaukee with her husband, Wilbur (1894–1963), in 1924 to help African American families obtain loans for the purchase of a home. In 1951, Halyard became the first woman president of the Milwaukee Chapter of the NAACP. The Halyard Park neighborhood in Milwaukee is named for Ardie and Wilbur Halyard. (WBHS.)

SECTION 45, UNMARKED GRAVE. Mabel Watson Raimey (1898–1986) was the last descendant of Sully and Susanna Watson (Section 16). Raimey graduated from high school at the age of 14 and was the first African American woman to obtain a bachelor's degree from the University of Wisconsin–Madison. She began her career as a teacher for Milwaukee Public Schools but was dismissed after three days because she was African American. (Department of Special Collections and University Archives, Marquette University Libraries.)

MABEL WATSON RAIMEY. Raimey did not let her dismissal from teaching deter her. While working as a legal secretary, she attended night classes and was the first African American woman to graduate from the Marquette University Law School in Milwaukee. In 1927, she was admitted to the Wisconsin Bar and became the first African American woman to practice law in Wisconsin. A historical marker on the Marquette University campus recognizes Raimey and her accomplishments. (AMP.)

SECTION 35 CENOTAPH. Alice Bertschy Kadish (1902–1998) was a kindergarten teacher for Milwaukee Public Schools, a community philanthropist, and a longtime advocate of fiber arts. Located in Milwaukee's Riverwest neighborhood, the Alice B. Kadish Memorial Weaving Center at Gaenslen School is named in her honor. Alice B. Kadish Park, overlooking the Milwaukee River and downtown skyline, offers summer concerts and bike and walking paths. (AMP.)

SECTION 33. With only a simple granite marker to denote her grave, artist Mary Louise Nohl (1914–2001) had a passion for creating sculpture, pottery, and paintings. Using found objects from the shores of Lake Michigan, Nohl filled her home in Fox Point, Wisconsin, with beautiful, unique concrete figures. Her home, the Mary Nohl Art Environment, is listed in the National Register of Historic Places. The Mary L. Nohl Fund, administered by the Greater Milwaukee Foundation, awards scholarships and grants in Nohl's name. (AMP.)

"DICKEY" CHAPPELLE. Dickey Chapelle (1919–1965) was born in Shorewood, Wisconsin, as Georgette Louise Meyer. She adopted the name Dickey after Arctic explorer Adm. Richard Byrd and later married photographer Tony Chapelle. Dickey was a daring and courageous civilian photojournalist during World War II, the Korean War, and the Vietnam War. She fearlessly photographed men in combat for *Reader's Digest*, *Life*, and *National Geographic* magazines. (Wisconsin Historical Society, WHS-1942.)

SECTION 33. In 1965, while on patrol with a troop, Dickey Chapelle stepped on a landmine and was the first female photojournalist to be killed in combat in Vietnam. Given a full military burial at the time of her death, she was posthumously given a Distinguished Service Award in 2015 and declared an honorary Marine in 2016. A Milwaukee PBS television documentary entitled *Behind the Pearl Earrings: The Story of Dickey Chapelle, Combat Photojournalist* features her life. (AMP.)

Section 6. Debra Lee Usinger (1954–2012) was a fourth-generation family member and the vice president of Milwaukee's Usinger Sausage Company. She was a civic leader, philanthropist, and strong advocate for the development of businesses on Old World Third Street and the creation of the Downtown Riverwalk in Milwaukee. She was recognized in 2011 with the Bravo! Lifetime Entrepreneur Achievement Award. (*Milwaukee Journal Sentinel*, © 2019 Journal Sentinel Inc., reproduced with permission.)

Debra Usinger Memorial. Supporters of Debra Usinger's involvement in the development of Milwaukee's Riverwalk donated funds to create a memorial in her honor in Edison Park. Created by artist Beth Sahagian-Allsopp and unveiled in 2014, the bronze tree sculpture, bench, and memorial plaque are just across the Milwaukee River from the Usinger Sausage Company. Usinger is also memorialized with the phrase "Smiles and Sunshine" engraved on her marker at Forest Home Cemetery. (AMP.)

Seven

Civil War Period

The Civil War (1861–1865) was supposed to be a short affair with few casualties. No one could envision a war that would last four long years and create a mournful cry in just about every Wisconsin home. Wisconsin provided 91,327 men to the war effort. Of this number, 3,802 died from combat and 8,499 died from other causes, such as disease or accidents. Statistically, 11.7 percent of the entire population served, with a death rate of 13.4 percent, still the highest of any war Americans have fought.

There was no national cemetery structure, and families were left to go to the field to bring back their loved ones. The government did not ship remains home. Consequently, almost half of all casualties lie in graves marked "unknown."

Forest Home Cemetery contains the remains of 981 Union soldiers. At least 11 more have been memorialized with a family cenotaph. An additional 33 were cremated or have been removed to other cemeteries. One such removal is Arthur MacArthur, father of Douglas MacArthur, who was buried at Forest Homc in 1912 but was disinterred in 1926 and is now buried at Arlington National Cemetery. At least 74 of the veterans buried at Forest Home died during the war and were brought back or returned home and died. Combat took 29 of these men, and disease took the other 45.

The federal government purchased a plot for some burials, but most were interred in family or single grave plots. Men from 27 states and territories are buried here and served in all branches of the military: US Army, state militia, US Navy, US Marine Corps, US Colored Troops, infantry, cavalry, and artillery, with ranks from private to major general.

As Gen. John Logan said, "If other eyes grow dull and other hands slack, and other hearts cold in the solemn trust, ours shall keep it well as long as the light and warmth of life remain in us." May they all, with the thanks of a grateful nation, rest in peace.

—Margaret M. Berres and Thomas A. Ludka

Section 24. During the Civil War, two areas in Forest Home were designated for the burial of soldiers who died in Milwaukee having no family, friends, or financial means to be buried with dignity. One site, known as the Soldiers Lots, contains 21 soldier burials. By 1863, "friendless" soldiers who died at Milwaukee hospitals and residences were interred in this location. Two men in this lot, Gordon Reeves and Benjamin Schubert, had Confederate service early in the war. Both men died in Milwaukee as Union soldiers. The other area is known as the Soldiers Home Lots (upper right) in Section 31. The Soldiers Home was established near downtown Milwaukee by the city's patriotic women, who knew it was more sanitary to care for the sick and wounded away from the battlefield and army hospitals. Fifty-two of the soldiers who were cared for at the Soldiers Home died "friendless" and were buried at Forest Home while the managers presided over their funeral obsequies. (FHC.)

SECTION 27. Pvt. Willett Greenly (1844–1862) was a young casualty of the 1st Wisconsin Infantry. His fellow soldiers took up a collection for the monument that stands in Forest Home. It reads: "This brave boy fell mortally wounded for his country and her constitutional rights on Sunday March 9, 1862." The monument also displays the moving sentiment "He was the only child of his mother, and she a widow." (MB.)

CHAPEL SECTION. Pvt. Francis Collins (1826–1930), at the age of 103, is the oldest Civil War veteran at Forest Home. He served proudly in Company I, 134th Pennsylvania Infantry. Later in life, Collins lived at the National Home for Disabled Volunteer Soldiers in Milwaukee. As gifted a storyteller as he was a landscaper, Collins became a celebrity as guests looked forward to visiting with him and admiring his beautiful site. (FHC.)

Section 19. Pvt. John H. Munroe (1833–1861), a member of Company D, 1st Wisconsin Infantry, was the first Civil War soldier buried at Forest Home. The family monument reads, "Died June 3, 1861. Drowned at Camp Scott." Unexpectedly, Munroe died in a bathing accident. After the funeral, his body was escorted to the cemetery by members of his company in a military procession. (MB.)

Lawn Place. Pvt. Charles L. Blanchard (1846–1942), the last known Milwaukee County Civil War veteran, lived to be 96. Blanchard enlisted in 1864 after turning 18, serving in Company D, 40th Wisconsin Infantry. After his service, Blanchard returned to Milwaukee and eventually became a businessman. He founded the Milwaukee Paper Company in 1883. (MB.)

SECTION 31. Lt. George Marion Bleyer (1840–1863) was a professional writer in Milwaukee. As a member of the 24th Wisconsin Infantry, he used his talents to write poems and letters describing the camps and battlefields, signing them with the pen name "Marion." These correspondences, sent to the local newspaper, were published to keep worried citizens close to their loved ones so far away. In December 1862, at the Battle of Stones River, a shell fragment wounded Bleyer in the knee. The errant fragment came from the 8th Wisconsin Light Artillery. A few weeks later, that injury took his life in a battlefield hospital. (Both, MB.)

Section 27. Capt. William S. Mitchell (1842–1863), while commanding Company D, 1st Wisconsin Infantry, experienced some of the most horrific fighting of the war. A panel on the side of the obelisk lists his major battles: "Perryville, Stones River, Chickamauga." Mitchell was killed in action on September 19, 1863, at the Battle of Chickamauga. There his company charged while the enemy attacked on its front and right. Mitchell was fatally struck in the neck by a bullet. At sunset, a temporary interment was arranged by Mitchell's men. After burying him in a shallow grave, one soldier drew a map of the location so the family would be able to bring him home. (Both, MB.)

Section 10. Pvt. Charles Mooers (1849–1864) is the youngest Civil War casualty at Forest Home, at the age of 14 years. In 1864, he enlisted as a drummer boy in Company F, 39th Wisconsin Infantry, but served only two months. Tragically, Mooers became sick with typhoid, which took the youth's life. His body was not returned to Milwaukee for final interment until 1867. (MB.)

Section 31. Cpl. Frank A. Hale (1844–1862) was the great-great-nephew of Revolutionary War patriot Nathan Hale. Young Frank served with Company G, 24th Wisconsin Infantry, and at the Battle of Stones River, the 18-year-old was killed in action. Hale was struck by a musket ball and died on the battlefield. When his body was recovered, the last letter from his mother was found in his hand. (MB.)

SECTION 32. Lt. Col. Charles A. Hamilton's (1826–1901) stately monument affirms that he was the grandson of Alexander Hamilton, first secretary of the US Treasury. The epitaph also remarks that he was "Lt. Col. 7th Wis. Vols. Iron Brigade. Severely wounded at Gainsville Aug. 26, 1862 while commanding regiment." At the Battle of Gainsville, Hamilton was the only mounted officer on the battlefield, making him a conspicuous target. He was shot in the right thigh by a rifle bullet that traveled through and lodged in his left thigh. Although the army surgeon tried, the bullet could not be removed. There it remained for the rest of Hamilton's life. Professionally, he was a well-respected lawyer as well as a distinguished circuit court judge from 1881 to 1887. (Left, MCHS; below, MB.)

SECTION 6. Pvt. Frank N. Fox (1842–1925) lived a long, successful life as a hat merchant in Fond du Lac, Wisconsin, after the war. While he lived a full life of 83 years, his impressive monument is a testament to the way he wanted to be remembered. The epitaph describes his service: "When the Civil War broke out in 1861, enlisted in the 24 Reg. Wis. Vol. Inf. Participated in all the battles in which his regiment was engaged. Was wounded at the Battle of Chickamauga, GA Sept. 19, 1863. Again severely wounded at the Battle of Resaca, GA May 14, 1864." (Right, MCHS; below, MB.)

SECTION 31. Privates Oswald (1837–1862) and Samuel (1843–1863) Kissam were brothers who served together in Company B, 24th Wisconsin Infantry. Oswald contracted chronic diarrhea, an illness that killed hundreds of soldiers. He perished at an army hospital near Nashville, Tennessee. One month after losing his brother, Samuel fought at the Battle of Stones River. He survived the battle only to die of disease in February 1863. One headstone, standing between the two graves, forever unites them and the memory of their sacrifice. (MB.)

SECTION 14. Pvt. Charles F. Webber (1846–1864) enlisted as a drummer in the 24th Wisconsin Infantry. While serving, he became seriously ill. After four months with no improvement, his father had the youth brought back to Milwaukee to recover. Even the family efforts failed, and Webber, just 18 years old, died at home. His parents had a drum carved on the family monument to honor their son's short life. (MB.)

SECTION 50. Cpl. John J. Miles (1845–1926) was born in Virginia and claimed the Fourth of July as his birthday. He was one of many young African American men who responded to President Lincoln's call to arms. Early in 1864, he enlisted in Company I, 32nd US Colored Infantry, at Lancaster City, Pennsylvania. According to his Grand Army of the Republic (GAR) war sketch, he participated in over 10 engagements. In July 1865, while fighting the Confederates at Honey Hill, South Carolina, he sustained a significant wound to his left foot. Despite his injury, Miles moved west after the war, making Milwaukee his home around 1880. He found employment at the luxurious Plankinton House Hotel and rose to the respected position of head waiter. (Right, MCHS; below, FHC.)

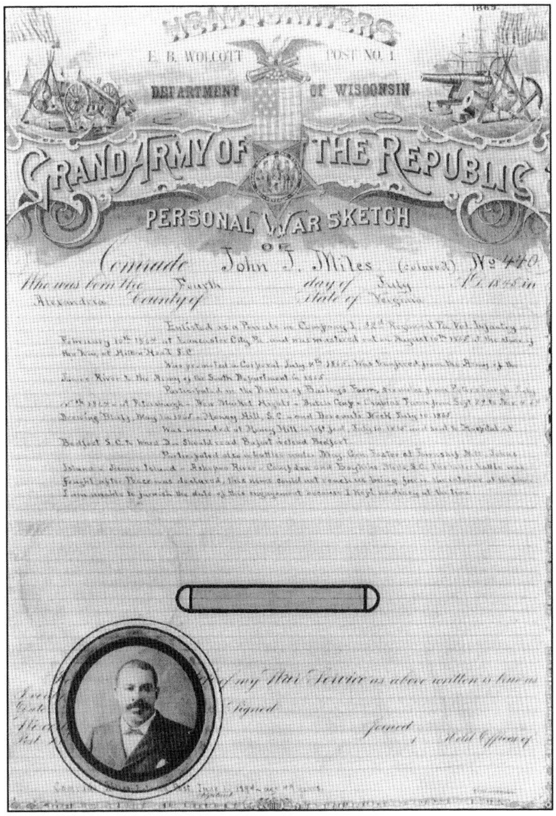

Section 34. Gen. Harrison C. Hobart's (1815–1902) heroic actions gave hope to Union soldiers at Libby Prison. He was one of those prisoners, having been captured at the Battle of Chickamauga while serving with the 21st Wisconsin Infantry. Hobart, with two other Union officers, devised a plan to dig an escape tunnel. After months of secret work, 109 prisoners crawled to freedom. About half made it back to Union lines. After the escape, Hobart continued his service, attaining the rank of brigadier general by brevet on January 12, 1865. Returning to Milwaukee after the war, Hobart resumed his established law practice and held various political offices in the city. (Left, FHC; below, MB.)

SECTION 25. Gen. Lysander Cutler (1807–1866) came to Milwaukee in 1854 and was involved in the grain and mining businesses when the war broke out. Since he had some military experience, he was appointed to the field staff of the 6th Wisconsin Infantry. Cutler was wounded in the right thigh at the opening of the Second Battle of Manassas. He was promoted to brigadier general and commanded the 2nd Brigade, 1st Division, I Corps at Gettysburg. His brigade was the first Union infantry to engage the Confederates in the field. At Petersburg, he assumed command of the 4th Division. After being severely wounded by shrapnel to the face at Globe Tavern, he was placed on recruiting duty and promoted by brevet to major general. He died in Milwaukee in July 1866. (Right, Civil War Photographs, 1861–1865, Prints and Photographs Division, Library of Congress; below, MB.)

SECTION 32. John A. Savage Jr. (1832–1864) initially served as adjutant of the 28th Wisconsin Infantry and resigned in 1863. He reentered the service in March 1864 in the 36th Wisconsin Infantry. In June 1864, he was promoted to the rank of colonel and led his men to Petersburg, where he was mortally wounded. He died on July 4, 1864. His grave lay unmarked until 2015. (JMA.)

SECTION 27. Capt. Fred Root (1831–1863) served with Company I, 24th Wisconsin Infantry. He led his company at Perryville, Stones River, and Chickamauga. Root was hospitalized with fever at Missionary Ridge, Tennessee. Upon hearing of a close friend's death and in a delirious fever, he died of a self-inflected gunshot wound. Together, Root and close friend Robert Chivas were taken to Forest Home in a December snowstorm. (MB.)

Section 16. Capt. Timothy Maynard (1833–1863) served with Company B, 63rd Pennsylvania Infantry. He was involved in the Peninsula, Fredericksburg, and Gettysburg campaigns and was mortally wounded at Rappahannock Station, Virginia, on November 7, 1863. His worn headstone reads, "Died from wound received at Kelly's Ford while in the act of giving a drink of water to a wounded rebel." He is Forest Home's "Angel of the Battlefield." (MB.)

Section 25. Adj. Garth Wilkinson James (1845–1883) was assigned to the field staff of the famed 54th Massachusetts Infantry. He was the brother of American novelist Henry James and psychologist William James. Garth was seriously wounded in the attack on Fort Wagner, South Carolina. After the war, he tried various business endeavors, married, and settled in Milwaukee. Unfortunately, he died at the age of 38. (FG.)

Section 19. Gen. Charles King (1844–1933) began his career during the Civil War as an aide to his father, Gen. Rufus King. Charles served with Gen. George Crook and was severely wounded by Apaches during the Indian Wars. He left active service and served as commandant of a Michigan military academy and developed the military science programs at University of Wisconsin–Madison and St. John's Military Academy in Delafield, Wisconsin. In 1898, King returned to active duty and was sent to the Philippines during the war with Spain. He remained in the Philippines during the Philippine Insurrection. Upon his return to Wisconsin, he was appointed brigadier general in the Wisconsin National Guard, and during World War I, he trained troops heading overseas. King is credited with writing over 65 books, short stories, and movie scripts. The city of King, Wisconsin, is named after him. (Left, MCHS; below, MB.)

Section 34. Lt. Robert Chivas (1842–1863) enlisted with his cousin John L. Mitchell and close friend Frederick Root in Company I, 24th Wisconsin Infantry. Root was the company captain, while Mitchell and Chivas were lieutenants. Chivas fought at Stones River and was wounded in action at Chickamauga, Georgia, in September 1863. He was killed in action while leading his men up Missionary Ridge in November 1863. His close friend Captain Root died the same day. A joint funeral service was held in December 1863, and both were taken to Forest Home cemetery for burial. Chivas was not a citizen of the United States but of Scotland and died serving his adopted country, as did many other immigrants of the time. (Right, FG; below, MB.)

Section 10. Pvt. Warren Graham (1842–1861) has the distinction of having the first military funeral in Wisconsin for a soldier who died of combat wounds. He was mortally wounded at Falling Waters, Virginia. The August 29, 1861, *Milwaukee Sentinel* stated, "Resolved, to die for one's country is a boon that is granted to but a few in proportion to the numbers who enjoy the blessings that good government confers." (MB.)

Section 40. Lt. William Lamberton (1844–1864) initially served with the 7th Wisconsin Light Artillery and was taken prisoner in Tennessee in December 1862. He was paroled and later joined the 36th Wisconsin in March 1864. Lamberton was killed in action at Cold Harbor in June 1864. His body was not recovered. He is one of 11 soldiers whose families have memorialized them with a cenotaph at Forest Home. (MB.)

SECTION 23. Capt. Otto Lehfeldt (1830–1898) enlisted in the US Navy in 1858 and served on several US vessels. He was memorialized when an incident he was involved with appeared in *Harper's Weekly* in January 1865. Lehfeldt was serving aboard the USS *Octorara* as a gun captain in Mobile Bay, Alabama. The *Octorara* was attacked by the CSS *St. Patrick*. Lehfeldt ran forward and grabbed the smoke stack of the *St. Patrick*, attempting to slow it down so the *Octorara*'s gun could be brought to bear. The *St. Patrick* exploded a torpedo in the mud beneath the *Octorara* that did little to no damage. The *St. Patrick* got away, but Lehfeldt became a newspaper celebrity for his efforts. After the war, he moved to Milwaukee, where his talents in shipping on the Great Lakes were in demand. (Right, FHC; below, MB.)

Section 9. Charles S. Hamilton (1822–1891) graduated from West Point in 1843 and served on active duty during the Mexican War, when he was wounded. He resigned from the army in 1853 and moved to Wisconsin. When the Civil War broke out, Hamilton was appointed colonel of the 3rd Wisconsin Infantry, and was later promoted to brigadier general. He was given command of the 3rd Division, III Corps, by Gen. George McClellan during the Peninsula Campaign in 1862. He was transferred to the western theater, promoted to major general, and given command of the 3rd Division of the Army of the Mississippi during the battles of Iuka and Corinth. Hamilton resigned from the army in April 1863. He returned to Milwaukee and became a US marshal. He is the highest ranking Union officer buried at Forest Home. (Left, WVM; below, MB.)

Eight

Wrap-Up

The previous chapters have only told part of the story of Forest Home Cemetery, and with a few remaining pages, Forest Home's historians would like to share some additional information.

The map on page 116 shows the layout of the cemetery, and it must be noted that virtually every road is curved. This was the original design by Increase Lapham, who laid out the first 72 acres. The section numbering system that evolved over the years at times seems to defy logic.

The largest monuments at Forest Home appeared between 1870 and 1910. This means that much of the granite and marble were brought by horse. Page 117 shows this effort.

The chapel, opened in 1892, was designed by the noted Milwaukee architectural firm of Ferry and Clas. It has two glass conservatories, one on each side, and had extensive floral displays into the 1950s. What makes the chapel unique is that in the basement is a crematory, the first in the upper Midwest, installed in 1896 with its own waiting room. Many of the early users of the crematory were from out of state and would wait while the cremation took place. It was also common for family members to help push the casket into the retort.

The pictures of the grounds crew from 1896 and today's grounds crew show how the nature of work has changed, at least staffing-wise.

On pages 126 and 127 are the listings of the many beer barons (chapter two) buried at Forest Home and the many mayors (chapter three).

Today, Forest Home offers many options for final disposition, including traditional in-ground burial, outdoor and indoor mausoleums, and cremation niches indoors and outdoors. The newest option is green burial, which is burial without chemicals using a biodegradable casket in a natural setting.

—Paul A. Haubrich

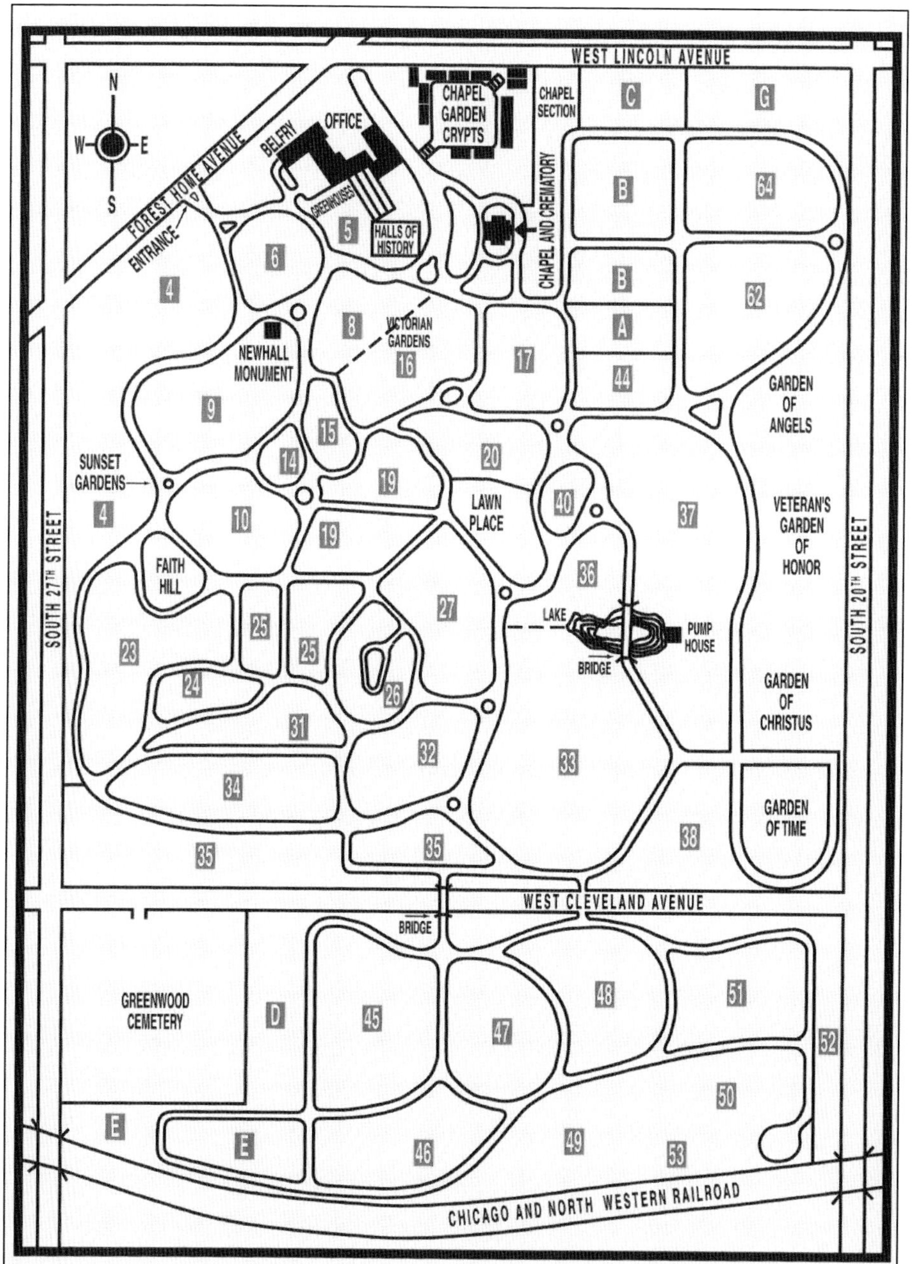

CEMETERY MAP. The Forest Home Cemetery map reflects the original intent and design of Increase Lapham. The garden cemetery respected the natural contours of the land as it was in 1850 with winding roads and a gentle rolling countryside. (FHC.)

Delivering Granite in the Late 1800s. An eight-horse hitch brings a large piece of granite, probably part of an obelisk, into the cemetery. Notice the extra-large wheels on the wagon to handle the weight of the stone. This was a common sight at Forest Home for years. After the Civil War, granite became the stone of choice and was brought to Milwaukee by train and to the cemetery by horse-drawn wagon. (FHC.)

Forest Home Bridge. The bridge at Forest Home Cemetery crosses the lake—actually a pond. Property with a lake view was a prized location for many, and just like regular real estate, commanded a higher price. (FHC.)

FOREST HOME CEMETERY CHAPEL. The chapel, designed by the Milwaukee architectural firm of Ferry and Clas, opened in 1892. On each side is a glass conservatory for floral displays. (FHC.)

CHAPEL INTERIOR. The wooden ceiling beams and glazed brickwork create a respectful environment. While intended for funerals, the chapel has also been used for weddings and community events. (FHC.)

CREMATORY. The first crematory in the upper Midwest was installed in the lower level of the chapel in 1896. It was oil fired and had two retorts. The room was elegant, with Corinthian borders and marble walls. (FHC.)

CREMATORY WAITING ROOM. There is also a family waiting room across the hall, as many families, especially from out of state, would wait for the cremation to be completed. Cremations take anywhere between two and three hours, depending on body weight. (FHC.)

1890s Staff. This photograph is probably dated around the late 1890s and shows both the fulltime employees and part-time summer help. The women in the picture were in charge of flowerbeds and greenhouse flowers used to beautify the cemetery. In the late 1800s, it took two men one day to dig a grave and prepare the grave site for services. (FHC.)

2019 Cemetery Staff. Current cemetery staffing to work on the grounds is about six fulltime staff and an additional five to six people in the summer to cut grass and string trim around monuments. This crew has to manage 189 acres, whereas the larger 1890s crew managed about 90 acres. Currently, one person using a backhoe can dig a grave in about one hour. (FHC.)

Chapel Gardens. Construction on this outdoor mausoleum began in 1956, and it has over 6,000 burials. Mausoleums became popular in the 1950s. (FHC.)

The Halls of History. The Halls of History is an indoor mausoleum. The lower level contains biographical displays of famous individuals buried at Forest Home Cemetery. Some of the individuals noted in this book and others can be found in the halls. (FHC.)

Cemetery Fountain. The fountain shown here was installed around 1900 and is a classic example of a Victorian four-tiered array with swans at the base. Note the extensive planting surrounding the fountain. This fountain would have been an impressive sight when entering the cemetery in 1900. (FHC.)

Original Fountain. By 1920, the iron fountain was replaced with a stone fountain built by the cemetery staff out of rock found on the property. This fountain is still there today. The floral displays surrounding the fountain are still there but are not quite as grand as the earlier version. (FHC.)

Section Prairie Rest. Prairie Rest is a green burial location at Forest Home. Green burials are a new innovation in cemetery practices. They do not use embalming chemicals, and the person is interred in either a cardboard box designed for this purpose or a pine box in an unmarked grave. This method is considered more ecologically friendly. A large rock at the entrance to this section is inscribed with the names of those buried here. (FHC.)

Victorian Garden. With the growth of cremation as a preferred option for many families, Forest Home has developed a Victorian garden-style setting using small columbaria to fulfill the needs of families. The Victorian garden concept reflects that age of the cemetery as a peaceful setting for final rest. This space was also designed to hold community events as part of the cemetery's commitment to community service. (FHC.)

SECTION 17. The gravesite of George Dittmar (1860–1913) is always a surprise when Forest Home Cemetery visitors encounter it. The tree and headstone have merged, with the tree gradually winning the battle over the last 50-plus years. This shows the power of Mother Nature to adapt and gradually become part of the story. (FHC.)

SECTION 19. One of the major design themes for Increase Lapham was to use the natural vistas of the landscape as it existed in 1850. The vista seen in this picture shows both the rolling landscape and the Victorian imagery highlighted by the obelisks aligned almost in a row. As noted in chapter one, the obelisk was a very popular lot marker for many families. Obelisks came in all sizes, with larger ones suggesting a family's success in the world. In the late 1800s, an obelisk depicted in this picture would have cost $750–$1,000, which was a lot of money. Similar-sized obelisks in today's market would run between $40,000 and $75,000—still a lot of money. (Both, FHC.)

Beer Barons

Name	Section	Born/Died
Charles Best	10	1812–1877
Jacob Best Sr.	08	1786–1861
Jacob Best Jr.	10	1817–1870
Lorenz Best	08	1826–1853
Henry Bills	33	1868–1951
Val Blatz	37	1826–1894
Fred Borchert Jr.	23	1845–1906
Franz Falk	33	1823–1882
Fritz Gettelman Sr.	33	1887–1954
Tom Gettelman	33	1917–2003
John Graf	04	1853–1930
August Krug	08	1815–1856
C.T. Melms	25	1819–1869
Richard Owens	25	1811–1882
Capt. Frederick Pabst	40	1836–1904
Gustave Pabst	37	1866–1943
Emil Schandein	40	1840–1888
Joseph Schlitz	36	1831–1875
August Uihlein	36	1842–1911
Robert Uihlein	36	1916–1976

MAYORS

Name	Years in Office	Section	Born/Died
Horatio N. Wells	1847	27	1808–1858
Byron Kilbourn	1848, 1854	24	1801–1870
Don A.J. Upham	1849–1850	Lawn Place	1809–1877
George Walker	1851, 1853	31	1811–1866
Hans Crocker	1852	31	1815–1889
James Cross	1855–1857	31	1819–1876
William Prentiss	1858	19	1799–1892
William Pitt Lynde	1860	19	1817–1885
James S. Brown	1861	27	1824–1878
Horace Chase	1862	08	1810–1886
Abner Kirby	1864	32	1818–1893
John J. Tallmadge	1865–1866	32	1818–1873
Harrison Ludington	1871–1872, 1873–1876	32	1812–1891
David Hooker	1872–1873	33	1830–1888
Ammi R. Butler	1876–1878	27	1821–1901
Thomas Brown	1880–1882, 1888–1890	14	1839–1908
John Stowell	1882–1884	27	1824–1907
Emil Wallber	1884–1888	23	1841–1923
George Peck	1890	06	1840–1916
John C. Koch	1893–1896	33	1841–1907
Sherman M. Becker	1906–1908	33	1876–1949
Gerhard Bading	1910–1916	62	1870–1946
Carl Zeidler	1940–1942	Chapel (in memory)	1908–1942
John Bohn	1942–1948	45	1872–1955
Frank Zeidler	1948–1960	Chapel	1912–2006

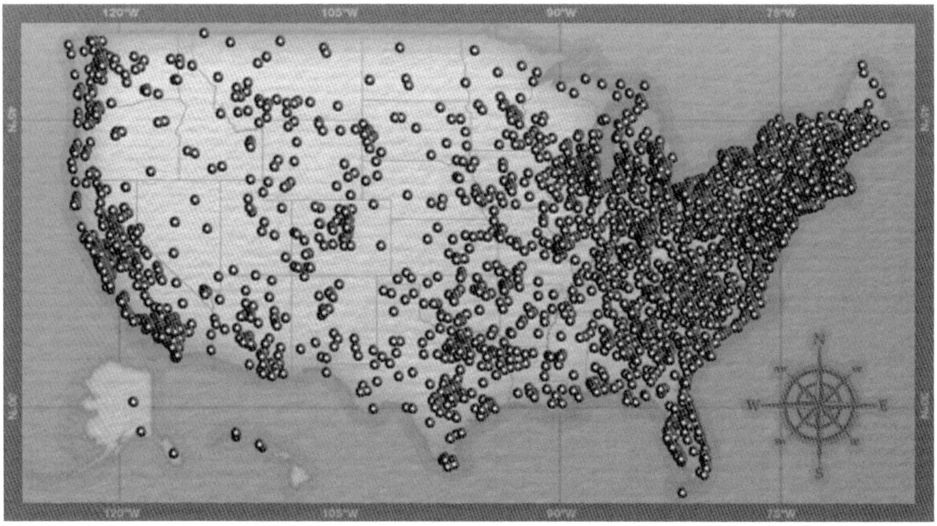